mary

writer
SEAN MCKEEVER

penciler
TAKESHI MIYAZAWA

inker
NORMAN LEE

colorist
CHRISTINA STRAIN

letterer
VIRTUAL CALLIGRAPHY'S RANDY GENTILE & DAVE SHARPE

editor
MACKENZIE CADENHEAD

consulting editor
C.B. CEBULSKI

sales manager
DAVID GABRIEL

collections editor
JEFF YOUNGQUIST

assistant editor
JENNIFER GRÜNWALD

book designer
CARRIE BEADLE

creative director
TOM MARVELLI

editor in chief
JOE QUESADA

publisher
DAN BUCKLEY

circle of friends

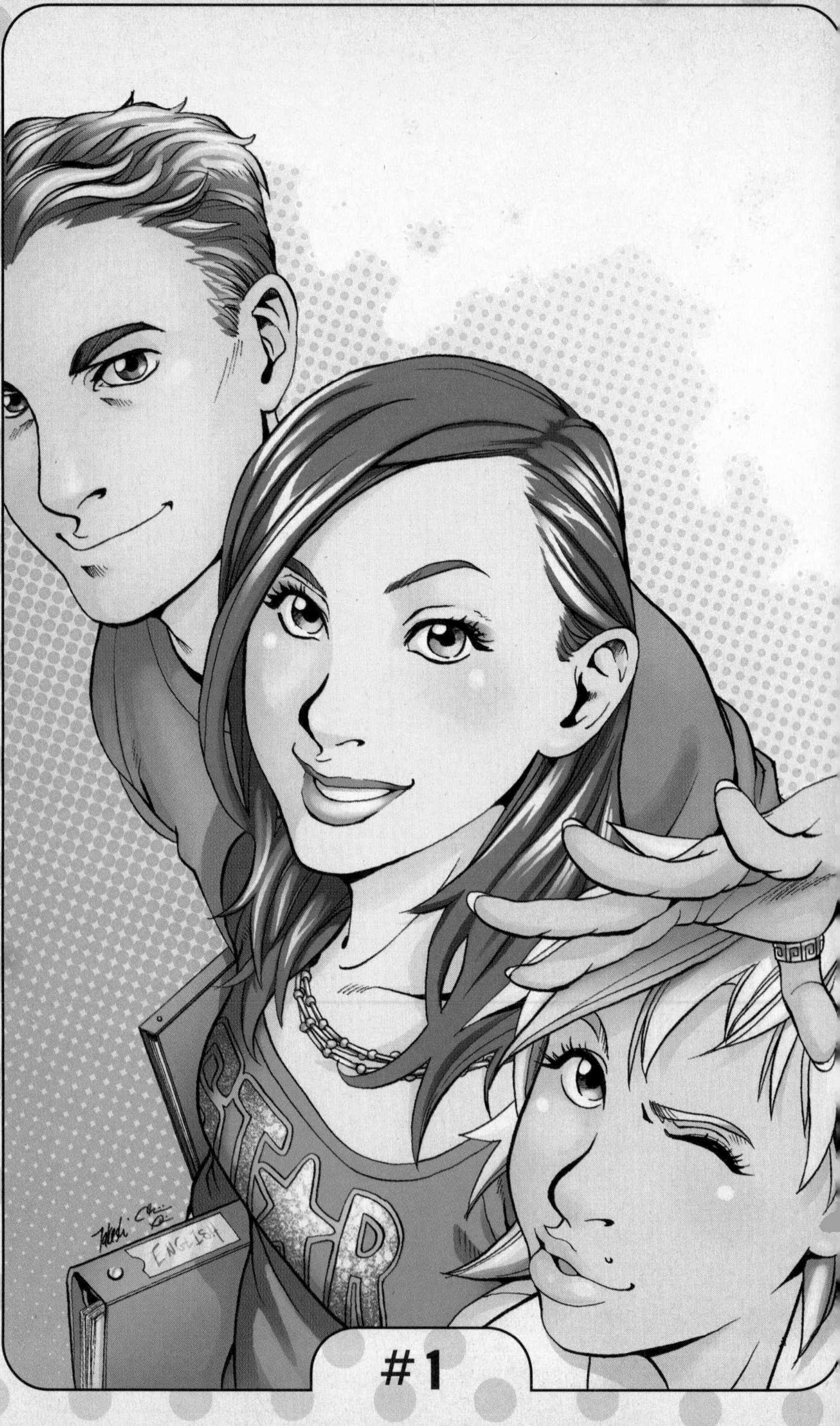
ENGLISH

#1

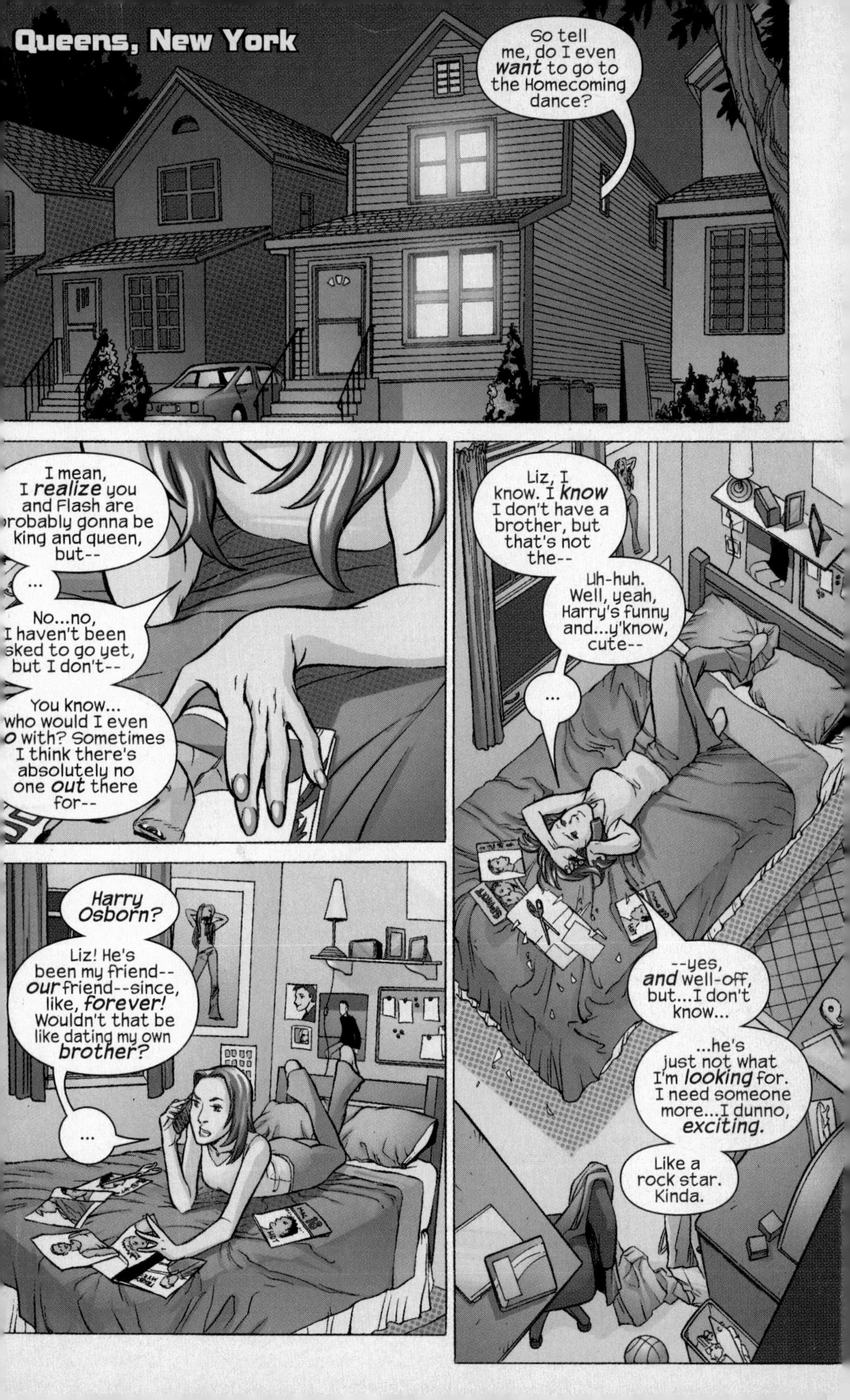

Queens, New York
So tell me, do I even *want* to go to the Homecoming dance?
I mean, I *realize* you and Flash are probably gonna be king and queen, but--
...
No...no, I haven't been asked to go yet, but I don't--
You know... who would I even go with? Sometimes I think there's absolutely no one *out* there for--
Liz, I know. I *know* I don't have a brother, but that's not the--
Uh-huh. Well, yeah, Harry's funny and...y'know, cute--
...
Harry Osborn?
Liz! He's been my friend-- *our* friend--since, like, *forever!* Wouldn't that be like dating my own *brother?*
...
--yes, *and* well-off, but...I don't know...
...he's just not what I'm *looking* for. I need someone more...I dunno, ***exciting.***
Like a rock star. Kinda.

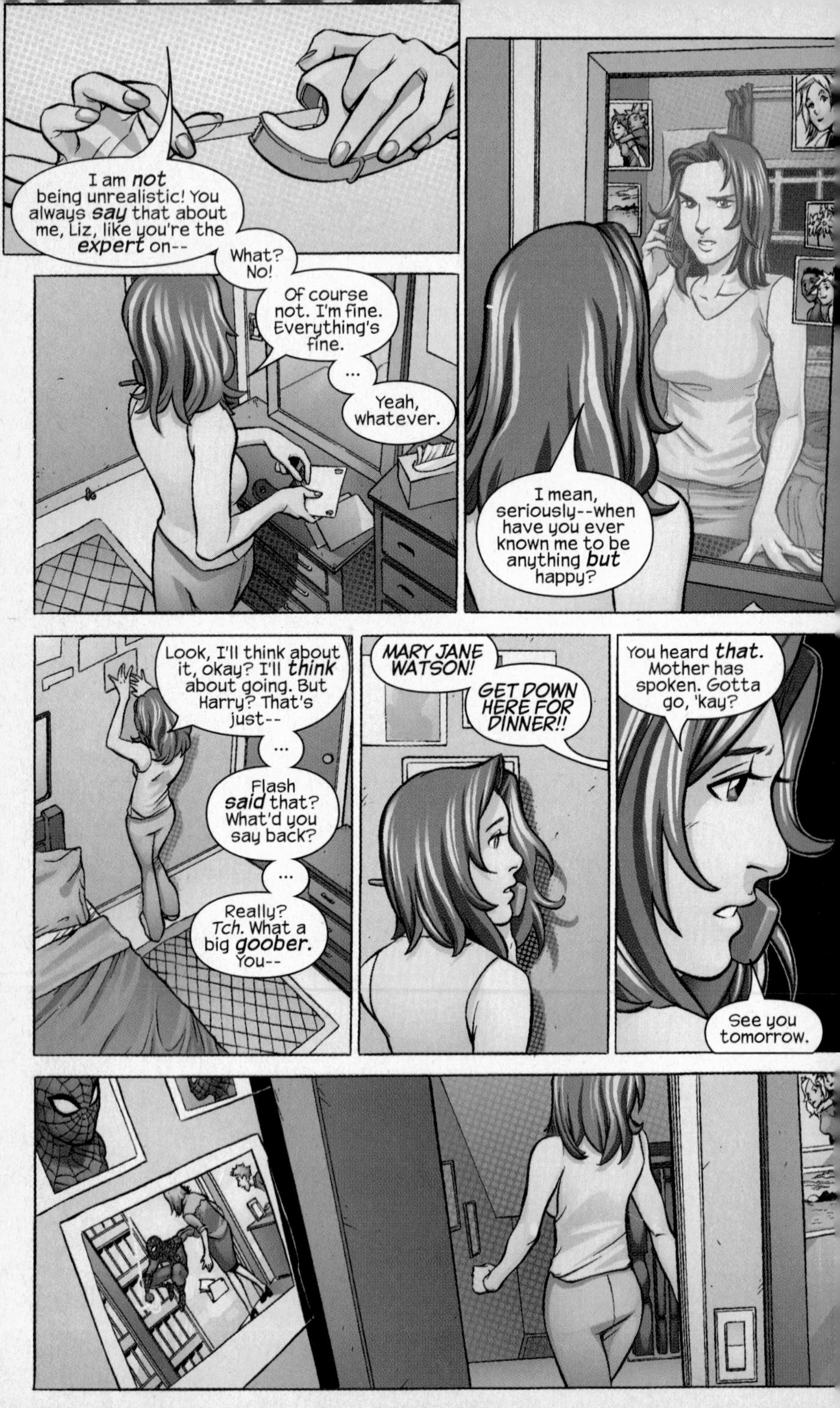
I am *not* being unrealistic! You always *say* that about me, Liz, like you're the *expert* on--
What? No!
Of course not. I'm fine. Everything's fine.
...
Yeah, whatever.
I mean, seriously--when have you ever known me to be anything *but* happy?
Look, I'll think about it, okay? I'll *think* about going. But Harry? That's just--
...
Flash *said* that? What'd you say back?
...
Really? *Tch.* What a big *goober.* You--
MARY JANE WATSON!
GET DOWN HERE FOR DINNER!!
You heard *that.* Mother has spoken. Gotta go, 'kay?
See you tomorrow.

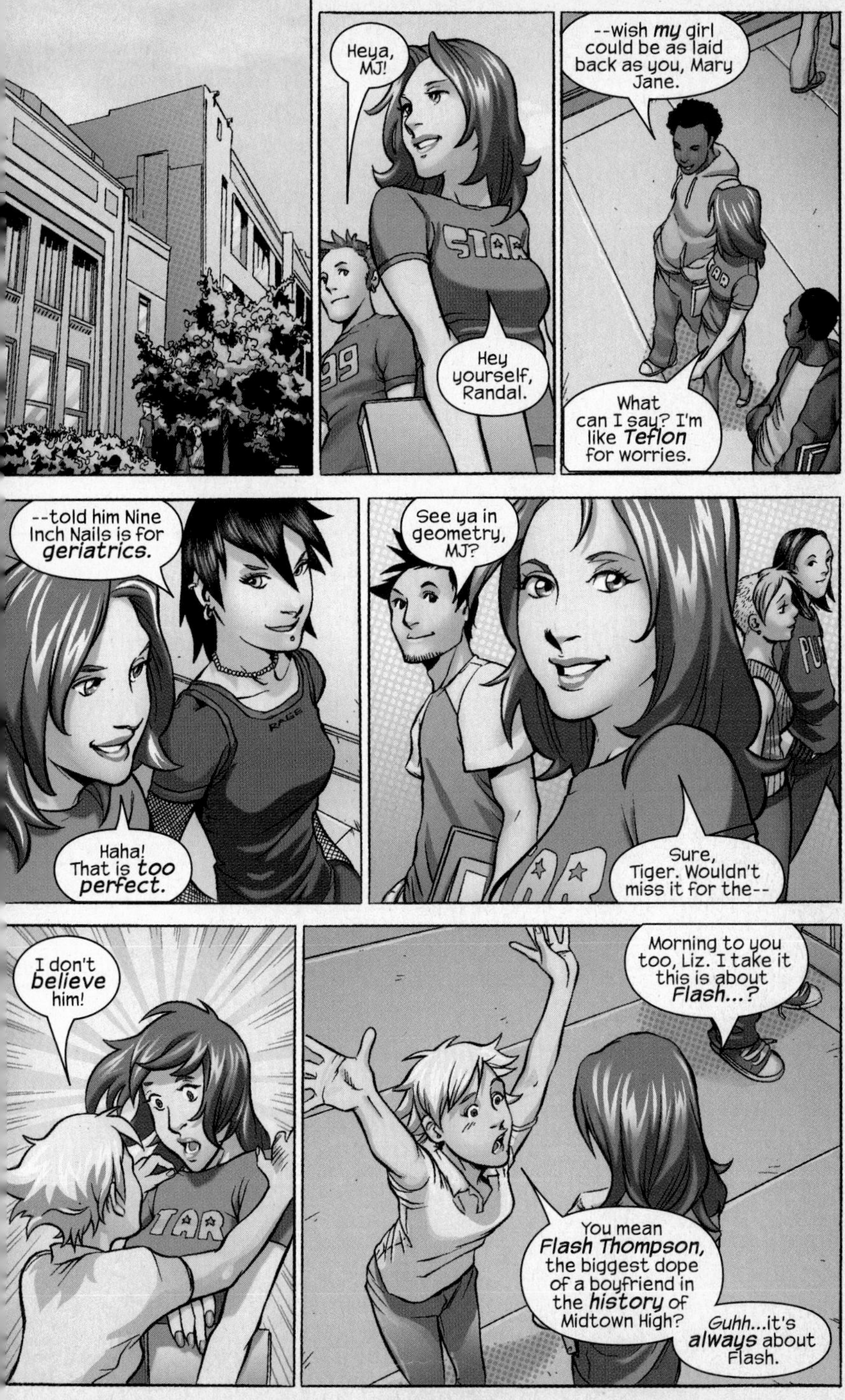

Heya, MJ!
Hey yourself, Randal.
--wish *my* girl could be as laid back as you, Mary Jane.
What can I say? I'm like *Teflon* for worries.
--told him Nine Inch Nails is for *geriatrics.*
Haha! That is *too perfect.*
See ya in geometry, MJ?
Sure, Tiger. Wouldn't miss it for the--
I don't *believe* him!
Morning to you too, Liz. I take it this is about *Flash...?*
You mean *Flash Thompson,* the biggest dope of a boyfriend in the *history* of Midtown High?
Guhh...it's *always* about Flash.

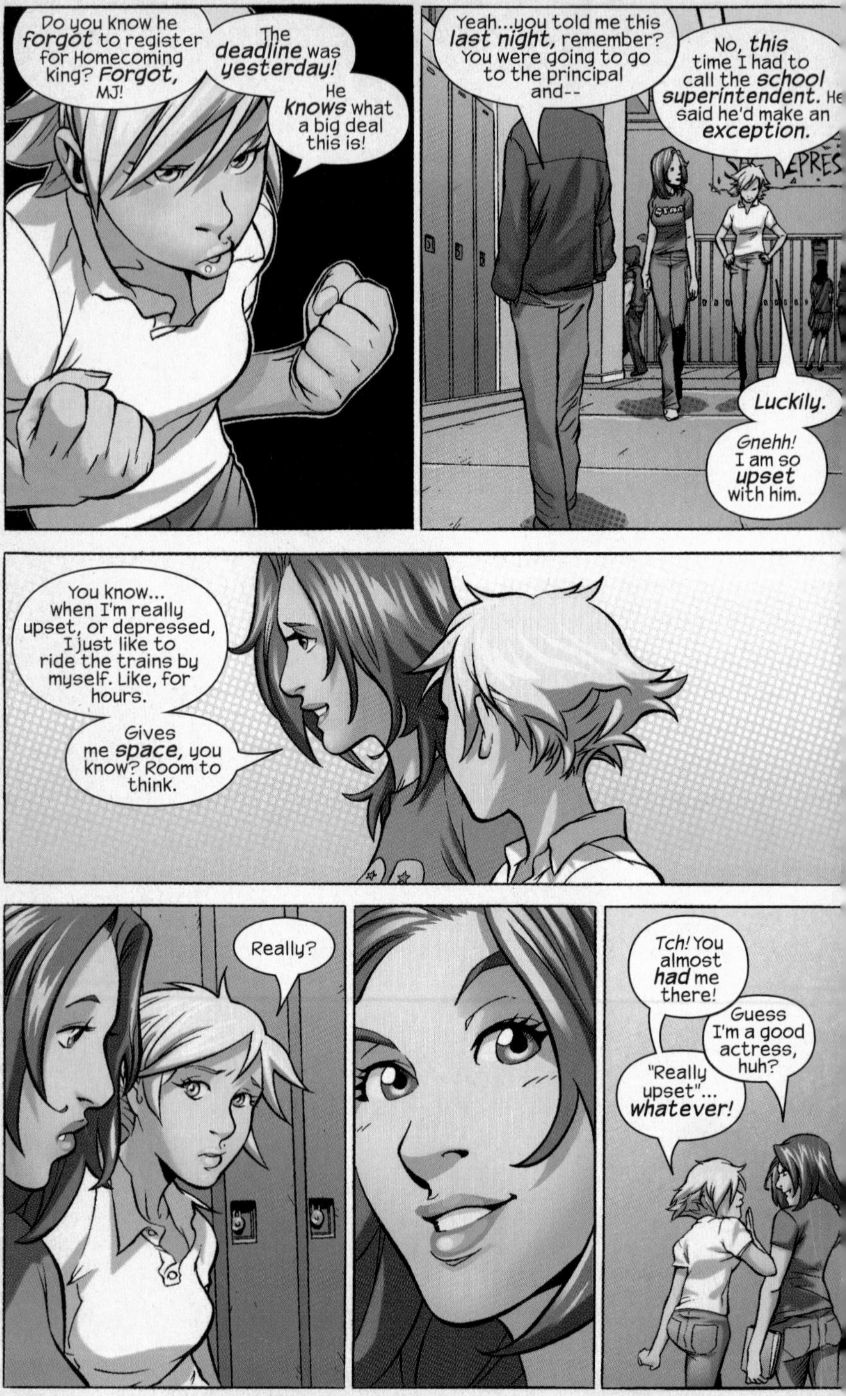
Do you know he forgot to register for Homecoming king? Forgot, MJ!
The deadline was yesterday!
He knows what a big deal this is!
Yeah...you told me this last night, remember? You were going to go to the principal and--
No, this time I had to call the school superintendent. He said he'd make an exception.
Luckily.
Gnehh! I am so upset with him.
You know... when I'm really upset, or depressed, I just like to ride the trains by myself. Like, for hours.
Gives me space, you know? Room to think.
Really?
Tch! You almost had me there!
"Really upset"... whatever!
Guess I'm a good actress, huh?

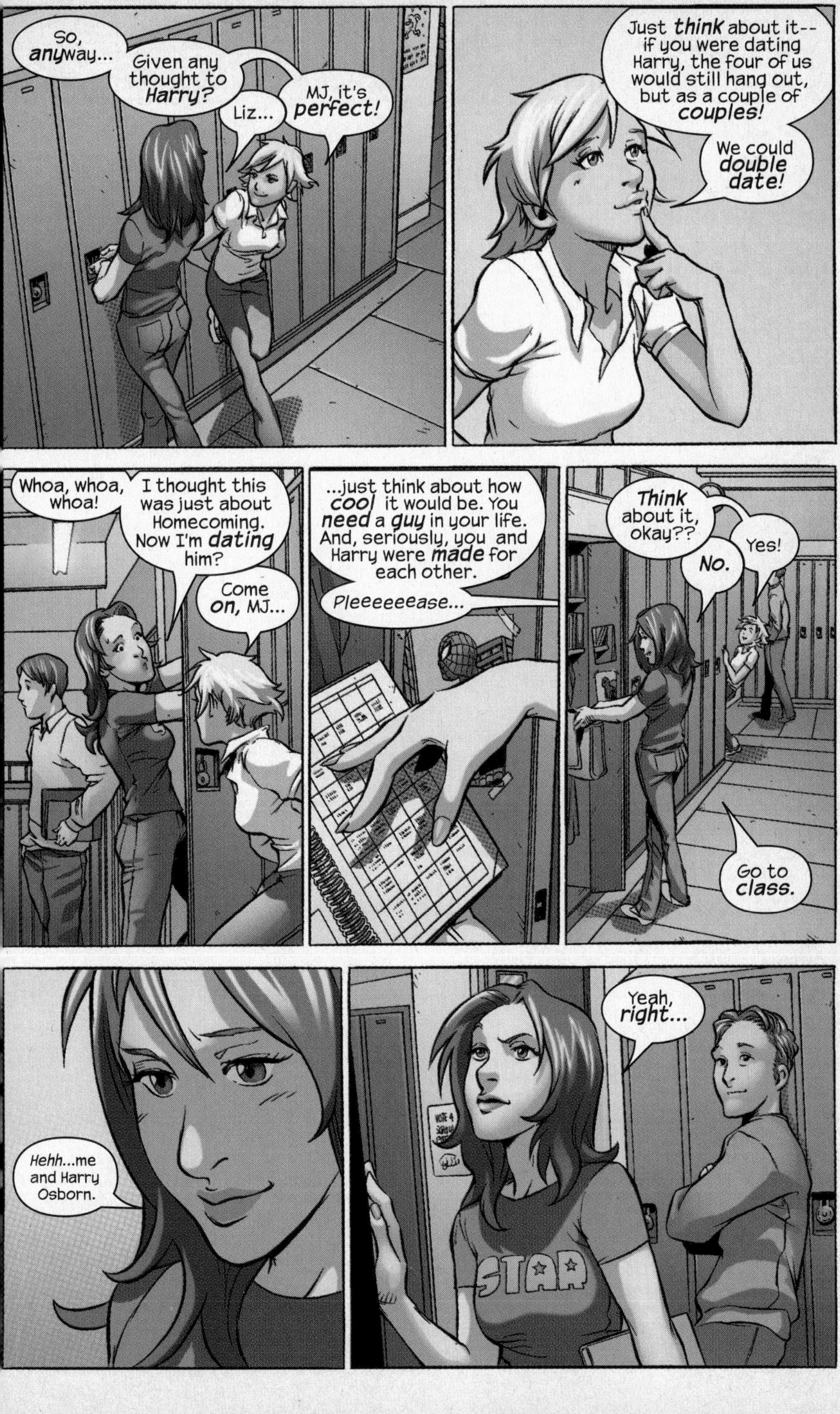
So, anyway...
Given any thought to Harry?
Liz...
MJ, it's perfect!
Just think about it-- if you were dating Harry, the four of us would still hang out, but as a couple of couples!
We could double date!
Whoa, whoa, whoa!
I thought this was just about Homecoming. Now I'm dating him?
Come on, MJ...
...just think about how cool it would be. You need a guy in your life. And, seriously, you and Harry were made for each other.
Pleeeeeease...
Think about it, okay??
Yes!
No.
Go to class.
Hehh...me and Harry Osborn.
Yeah, right...
STAR

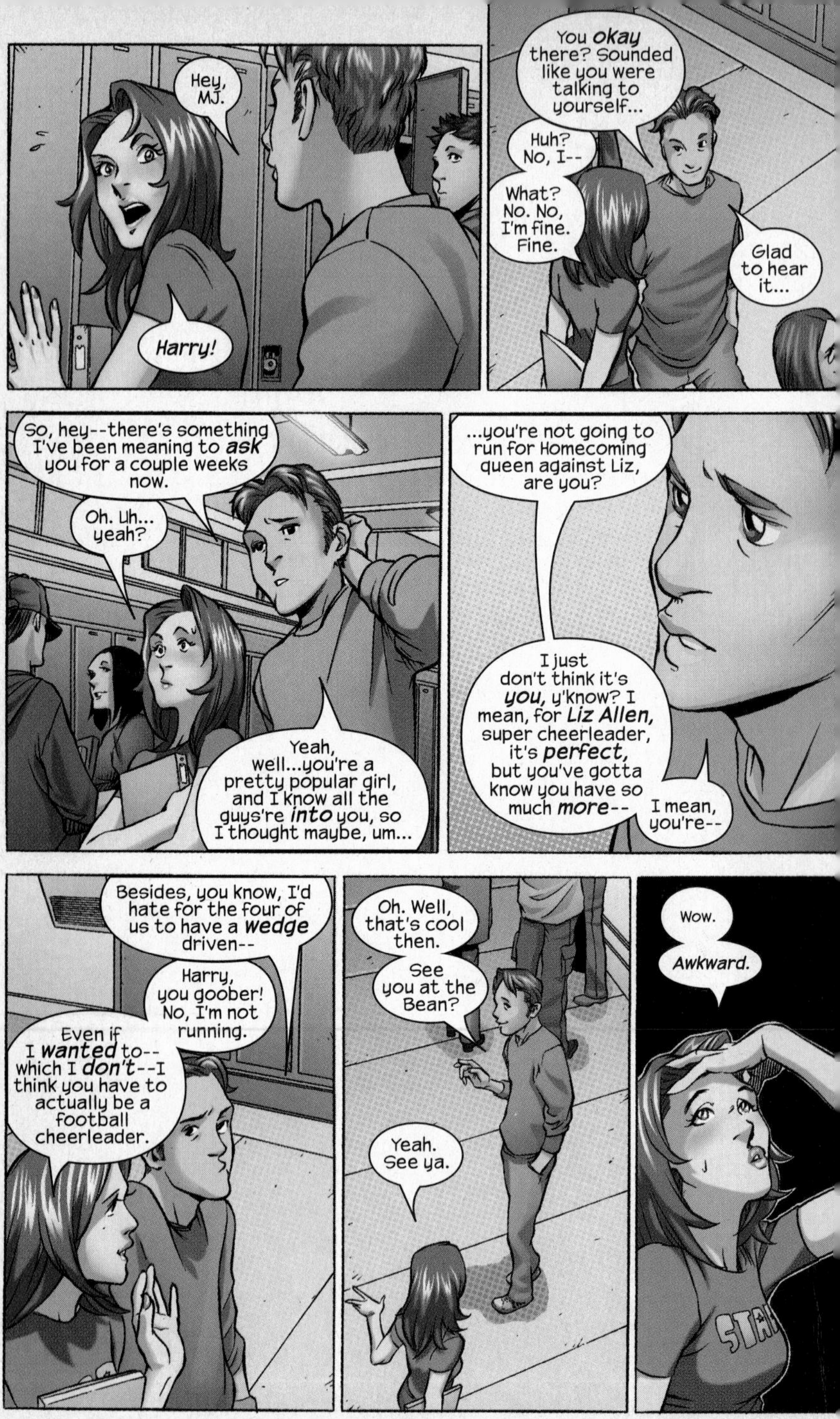
Hey, MJ.
Harry!
You okay there? Sounded like you were talking to yourself...
Huh? No, I--
What? No. No, I'm fine. Fine.
Glad to hear it...
So, hey--there's something I've been meaning to ask you for a couple weeks now.
Oh. Uh... yeah?
Yeah, well...you're a pretty popular girl, and I know all the guys're into you, so I thought maybe, um...
...you're not going to run for Homecoming queen against Liz, are you?
I just don't think it's you, y'know? I mean, for Liz Allen, super cheerleader, it's perfect, but you've gotta know you have so much more--
I mean, you're--
Besides, you know, I'd hate for the four of us to have a wedge driven--
Harry, you goober! No, I'm not running.
Even if I wanted to--which I don't--I think you have to actually be a football cheerleader.
Oh. Well, that's cool then.
See you at the Bean?
Yeah. See ya.
Wow.
Awkward.

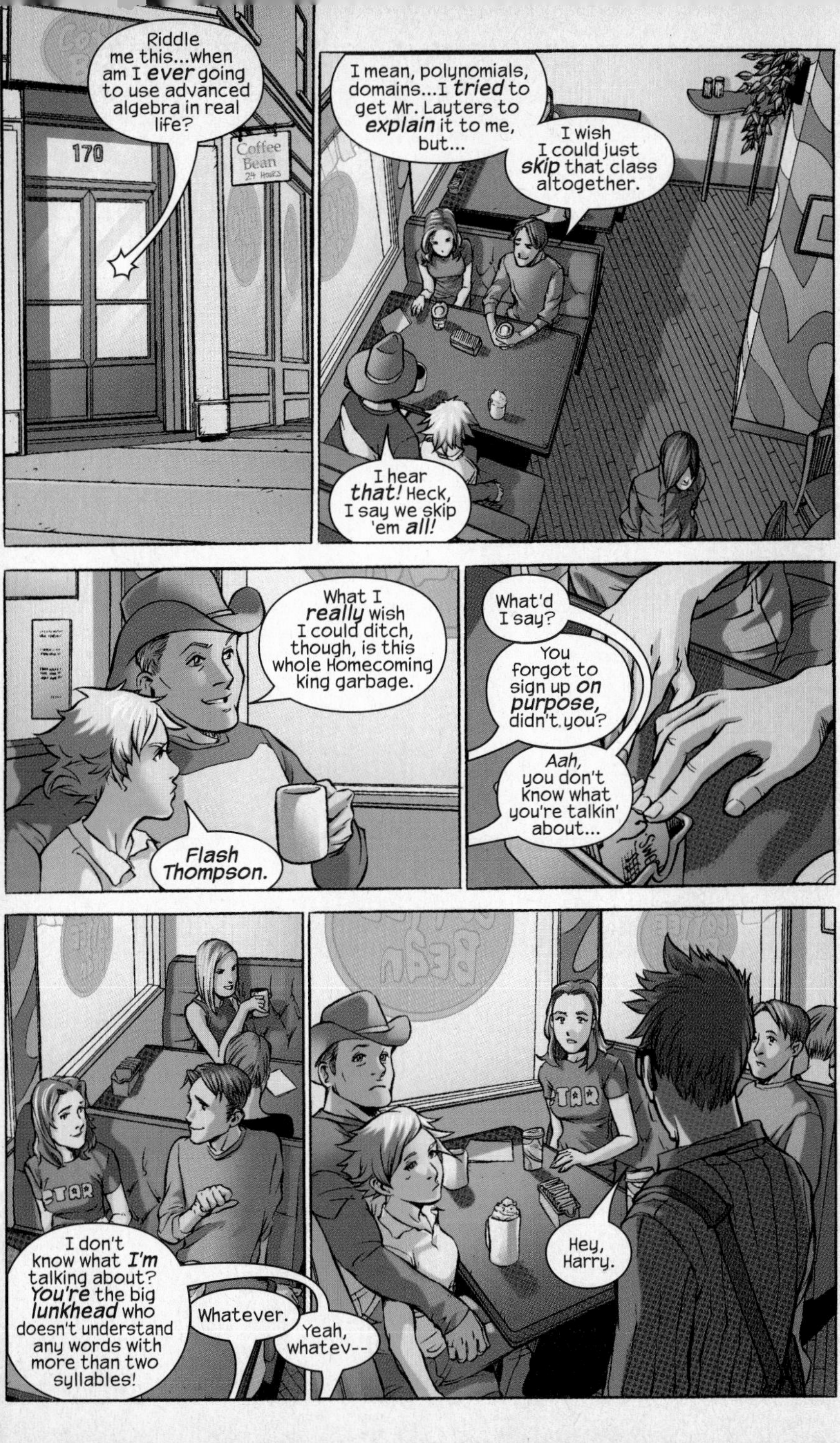
Riddle me this...when am I ever going to use advanced algebra in real life?
170
Coffee Bean 24 HOURS
I mean, polynomials, domains...I tried to get Mr. Layters to explain it to me, but...
I wish I could just skip that class altogether.
I hear that! Heck, I say we skip 'em all!
What I really wish I could ditch, though, is this whole Homecoming King garbage.
Flash Thompson.
What'd I say?
You forgot to sign up on purpose, didn't you?
Aah, you don't know what you're talkin' about...
I don't know what I'm talking about? You're the big lunkhead who doesn't understand any words with more than two syllables!
Whatever.
Yeah, whatev--
Hey, Harry.

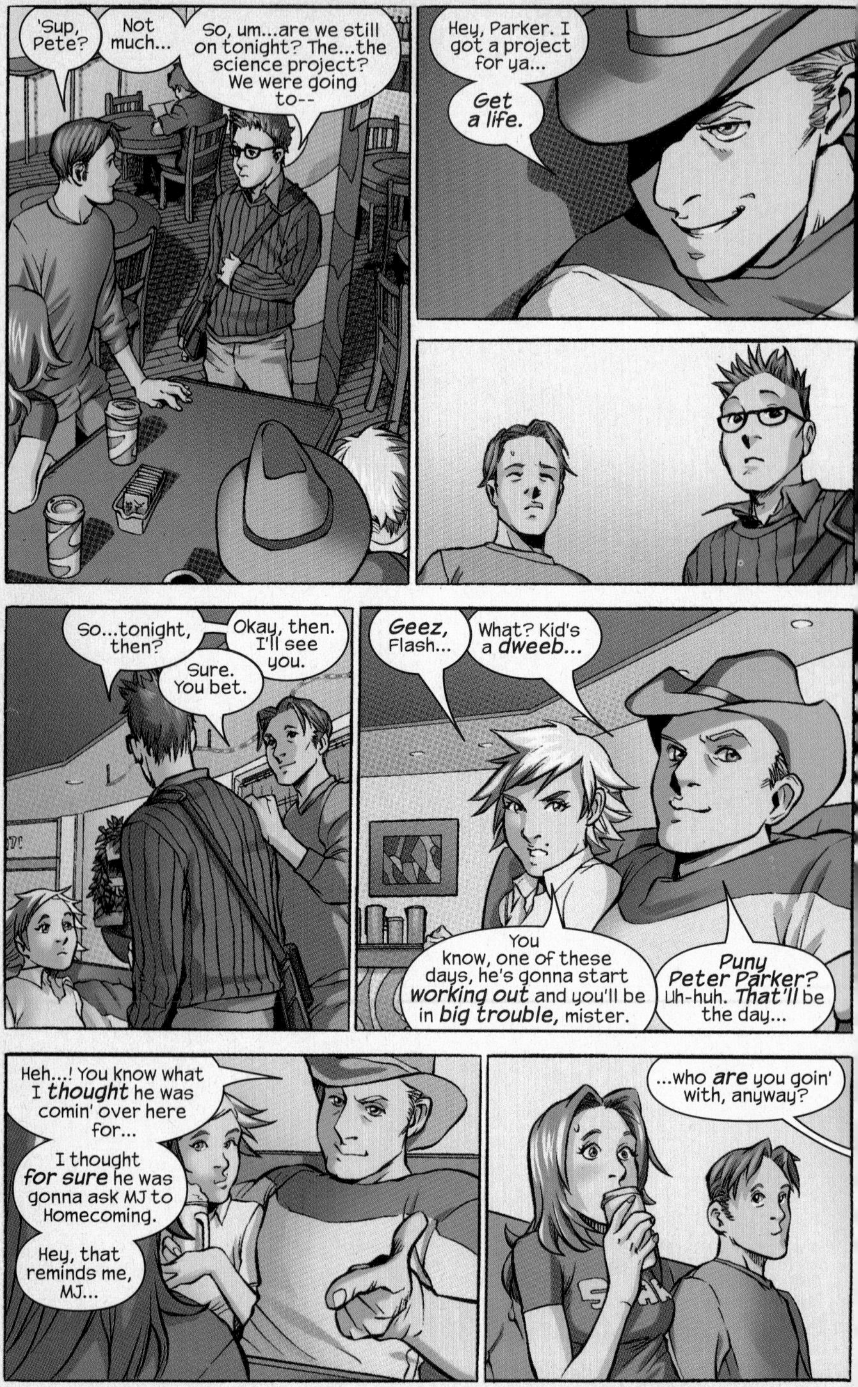
'Sup, Pete?
Not much...
So, um...are we still on tonight? The...the science project? We were going to--
Hey, Parker. I got a project for ya...
Get a life.
So...tonight, then?
Okay, then. I'll see you.
Sure. You bet.
Geez, Flash...
What? Kid's a dweeb...
You know, one of these days, he's gonna start working out and you'll be in big trouble, mister.
Puny Peter Parker? Uh-huh. That'll be the day...
Heh...! You know what I thought he was comin' over here for...
I thought for sure he was gonna ask MJ to Homecoming.
Hey, that reminds me, MJ...
...who are you goin' with, anyway?

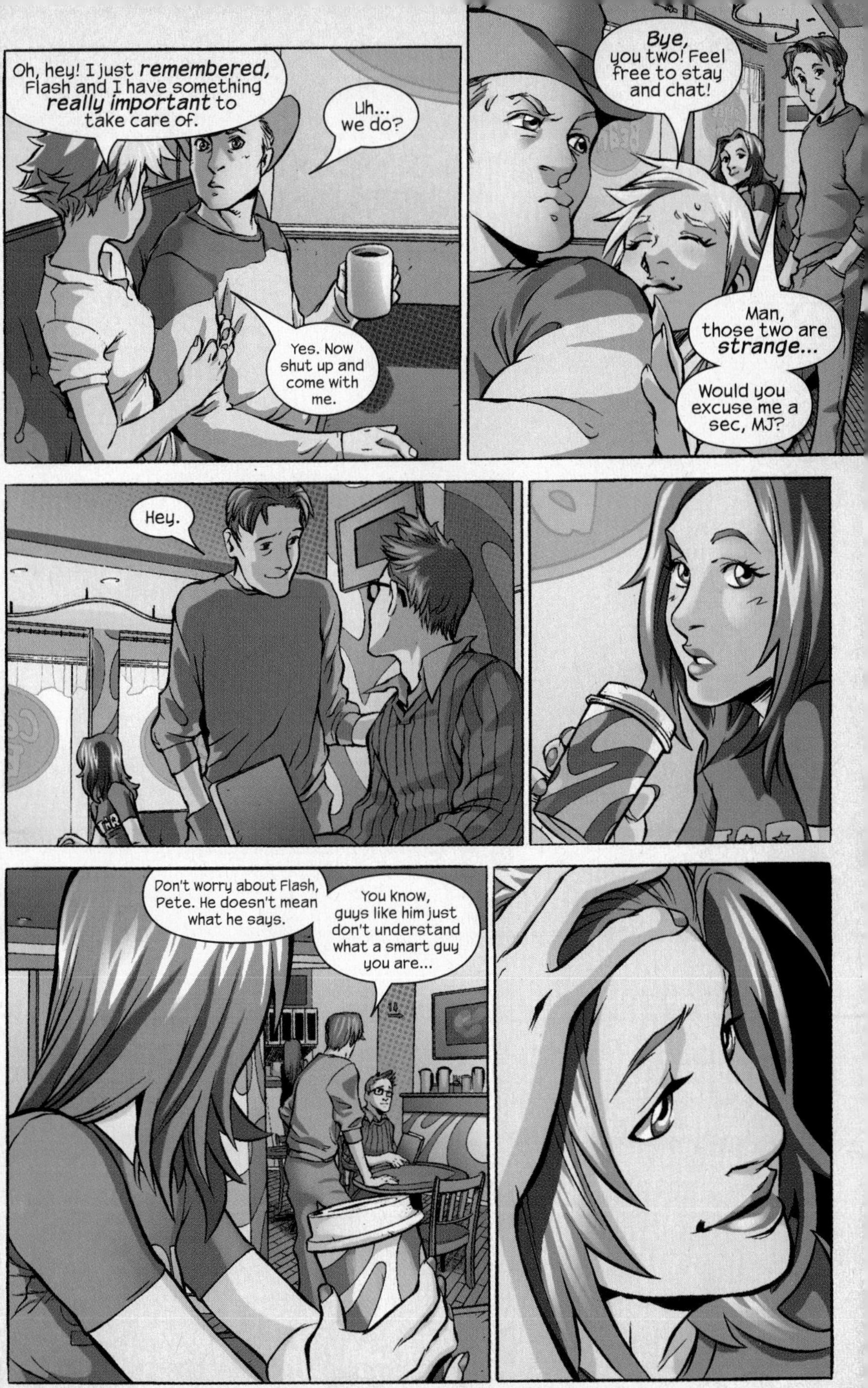
Oh, hey! I just *remembered,* Flash and I have something *really important* to take care of.
Uh... we do?
Yes. Now shut up and come with me.
Bye, you two! Feel free to stay and chat!
Man, those two are *strange...*
Would you excuse me a sec, MJ?
Hey.
Don't worry about Flash, Pete. He doesn't mean what he says.
You know, guys like him just don't understand what a smart guy you are...

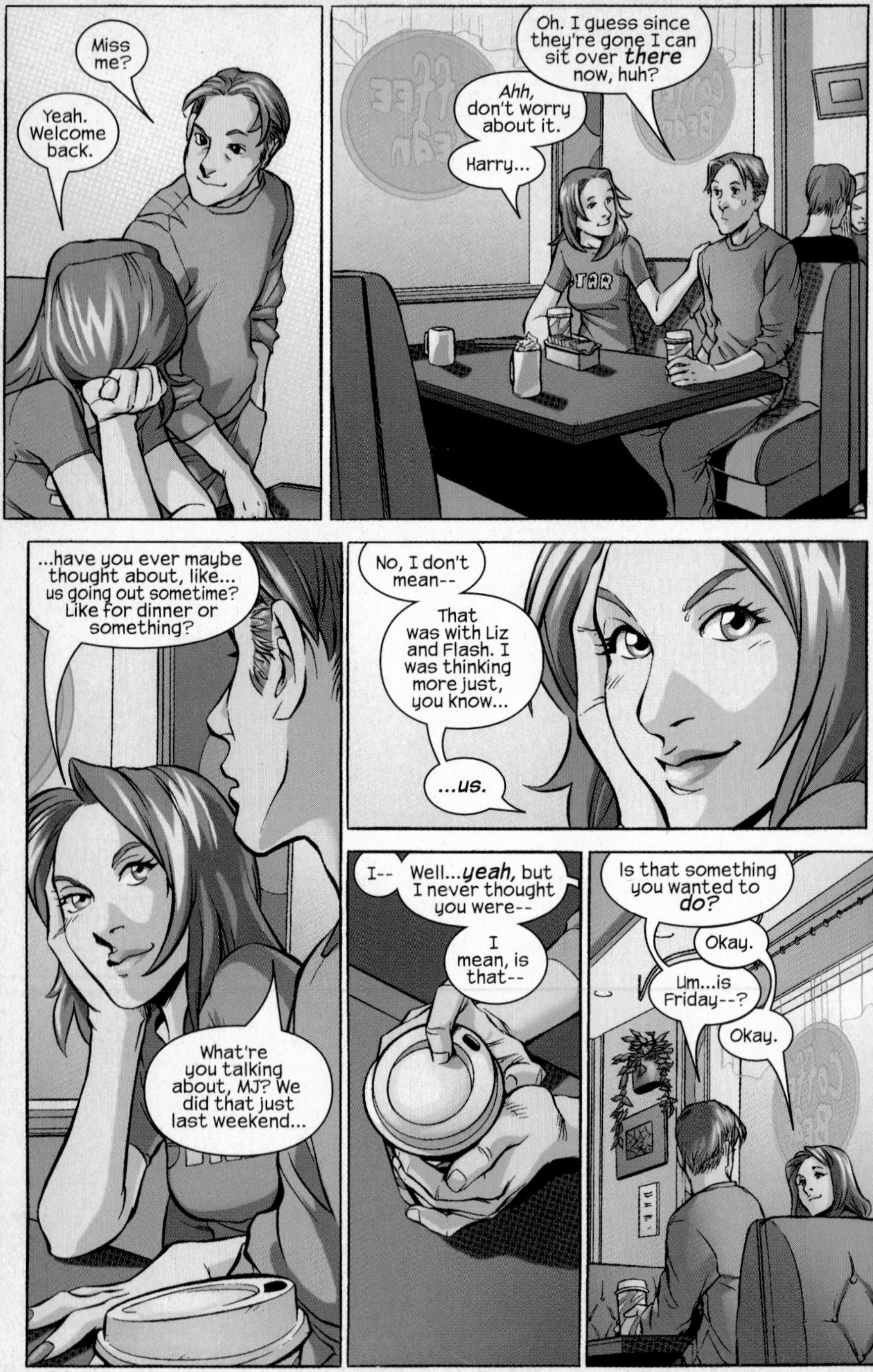
Miss me?
Yeah. Welcome back.
Oh. I guess since they're gone I can sit over *there* now, huh?
Ahh, don't worry about it.
Harry...
...have you ever maybe thought about, like... us going out sometime? Like for dinner or something?
What're you talking about, MJ? We did that just last weekend...
No, I don't mean--
That was with Liz and Flash. I was thinking more just, you know...
...us.
I--
Well...*yeah,* but I never thought you were--
I mean, is that--
Is that something you wanted to *do?*
Okay.
Um...is Friday--?
Okay.

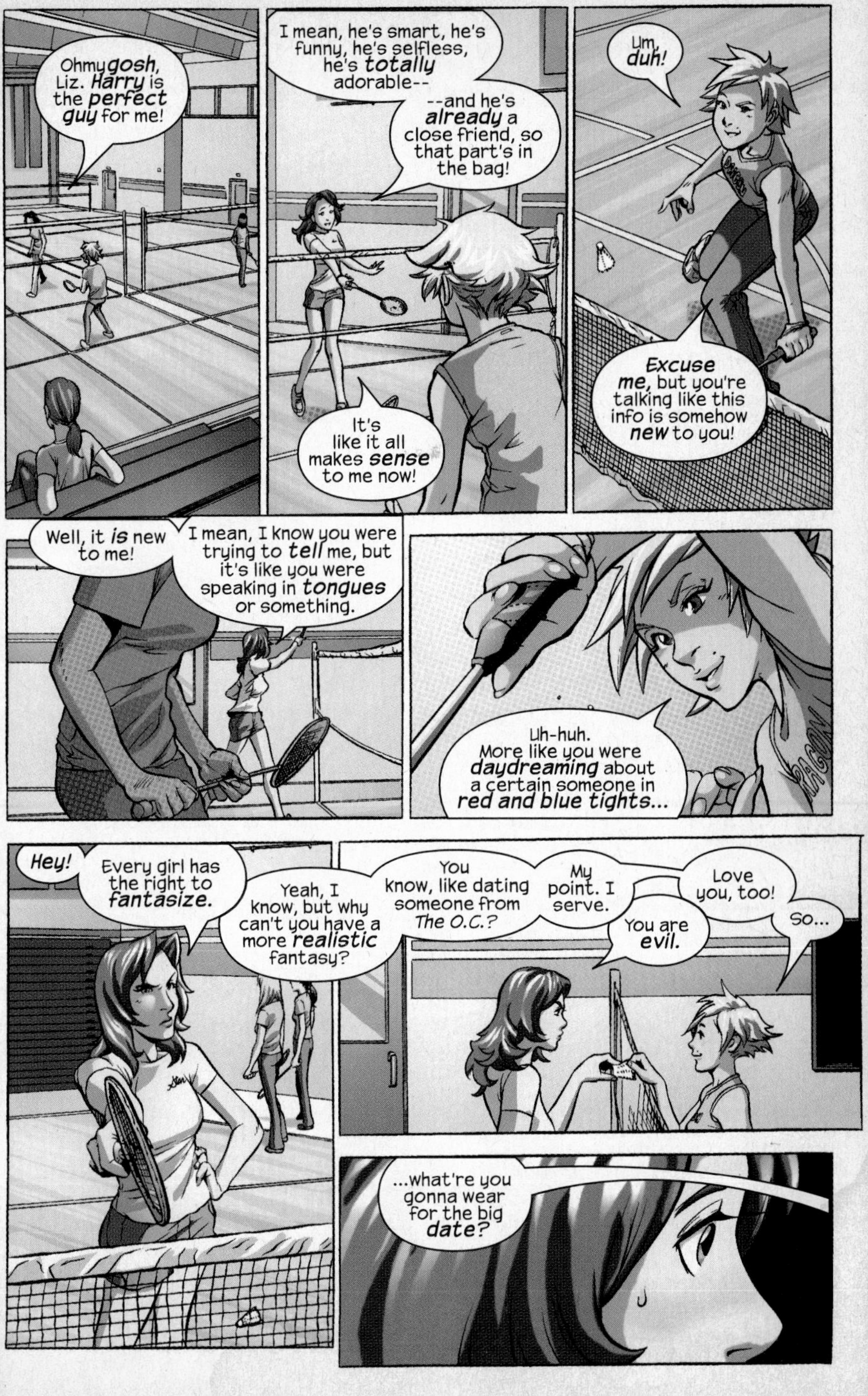
Ohmygosh, Liz. Harry is the perfect guy for me!
I mean, he's smart, he's funny, he's selfless, he's totally adorable--
--and he's already a close friend, so that part's in the bag!
It's like it all makes sense to me now!
Um, duh!
Excuse me, but you're talking like this info is somehow new to you!
Well, it is new to me!
I mean, I know you were trying to tell me, but it's like you were speaking in tongues or something.
Uh-huh. More like you were daydreaming about a certain someone in red and blue tights...
Hey!
Every girl has the right to fantasize.
Yeah, I know, but why can't you have a more realistic fantasy?
You know, like dating someone from The O.C.?
My point. I serve.
You are evil.
Love you, too!
So...
...what're you gonna wear for the big date?

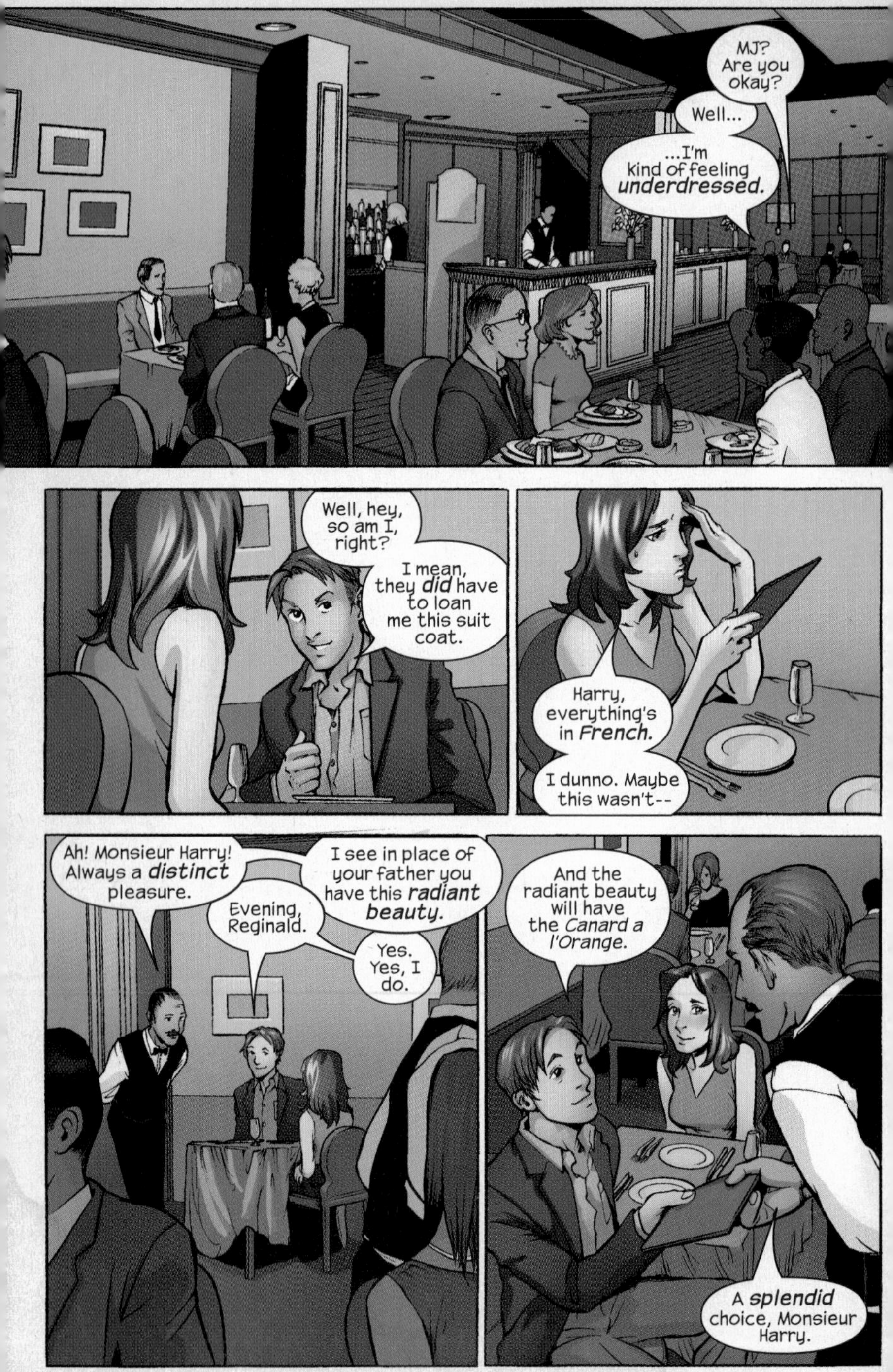
MJ? Are you okay?
Well...
...I'm kind of feeling *underdressed.*
Well, hey, so am I, right?
I mean, they *did* have to loan me this suit coat.
Harry, everything's in *French.*
I dunno. Maybe this wasn't--
Ah! Monsieur Harry! Always a *distinct* pleasure.
Evening, Reginald.
I see in place of your father you have this *radiant beauty.*
Yes. Yes, I do.
And the radiant beauty will have the *Canard a l'Orange.*
A *splendid* choice, Monsieur Harry.

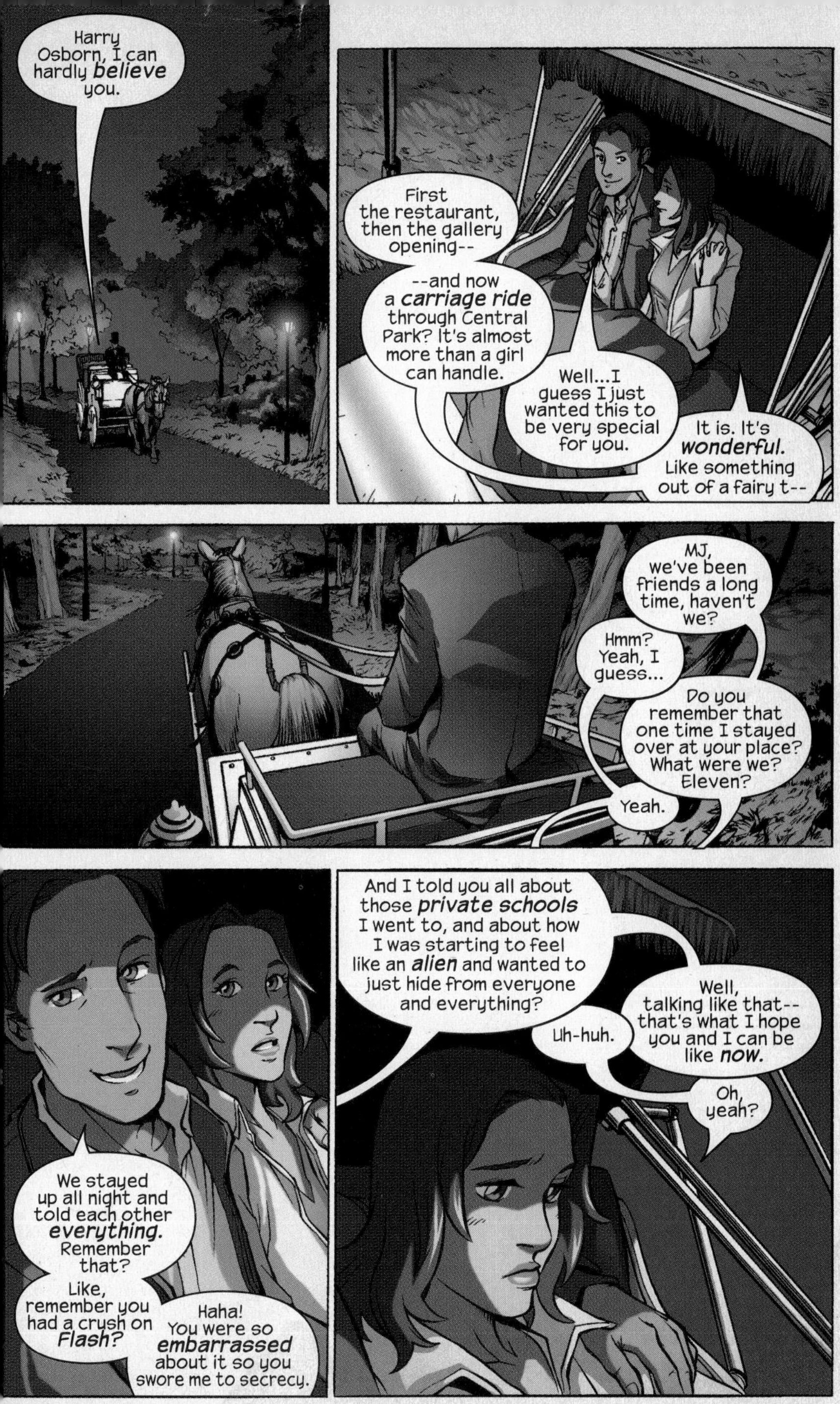
Harry Osborn, I can hardly *believe* you.
First the restaurant, then the gallery opening--
--and now a *carriage ride* through Central Park? It's almost more than a girl can handle.
Well...I guess I just wanted this to be very special for you.
It is. It's *wonderful.* Like something out of a fairy t--
MJ, we've been friends a long time, haven't we?
Hmm? Yeah, I guess...
Do you remember that one time I stayed over at your place? What were we? Eleven?
Yeah.
We stayed up all night and told each other *everything.* Remember that?
Like, remember you had a crush on *Flash?*
Haha! You were so *embarrassed* about it so you swore me to secrecy.
And I told you all about those *private schools* I went to, and about how I was starting to feel like an *alien* and wanted to just hide from everyone and everything?
Uh-huh.
Well, talking like that--that's what I hope you and I can be like *now.*
Oh, yeah?

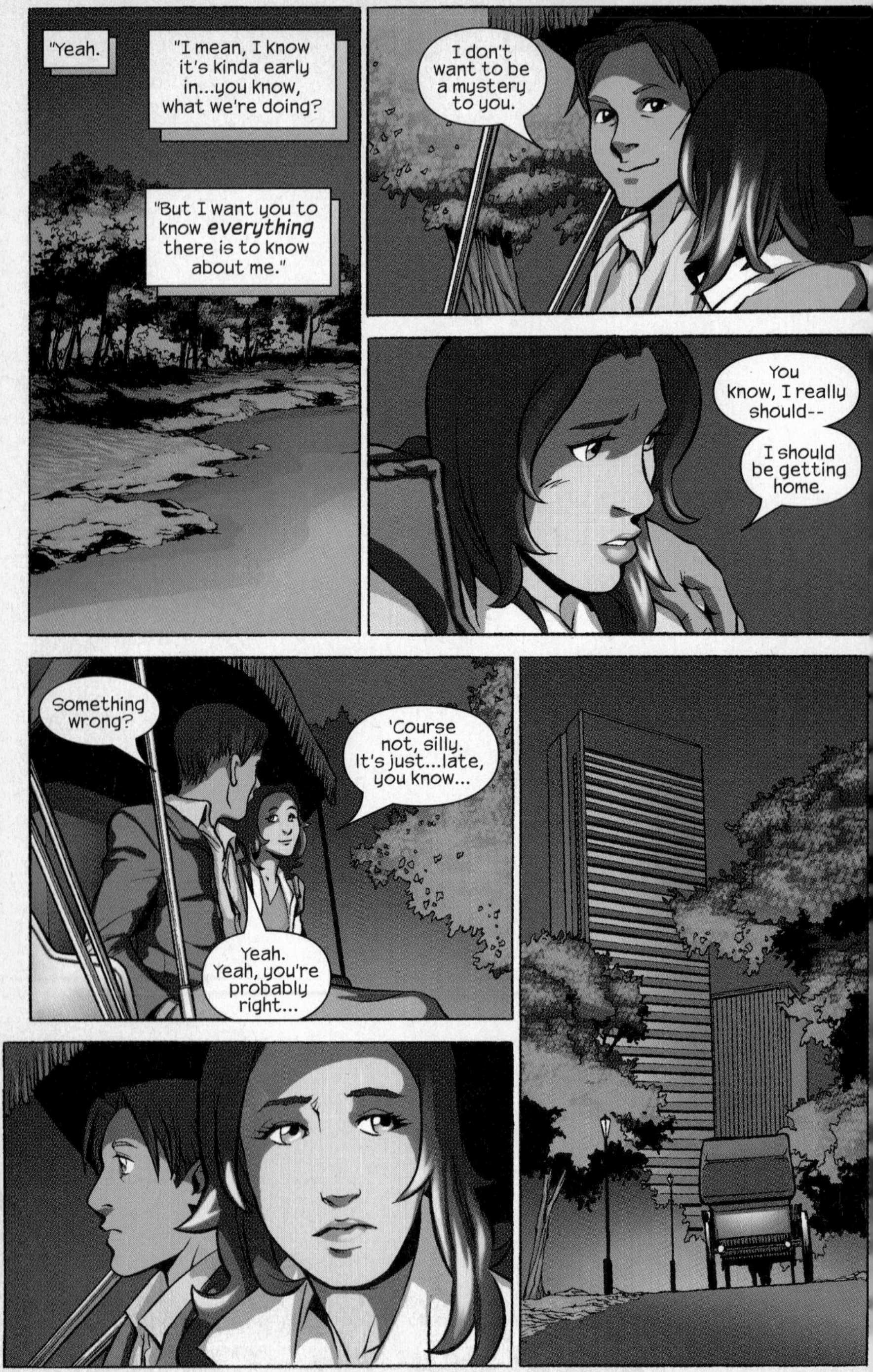
"Yeah.
"I mean, I know it's kinda early in...you know, what we're doing?
"But I want you to know *everything* there is to know about me."
I don't want to be a mystery to you.
You know, I really should--
I should be getting home.
Something wrong?
'Course not, silly. It's just...late, you know...
Yeah. Yeah, you're probably right...

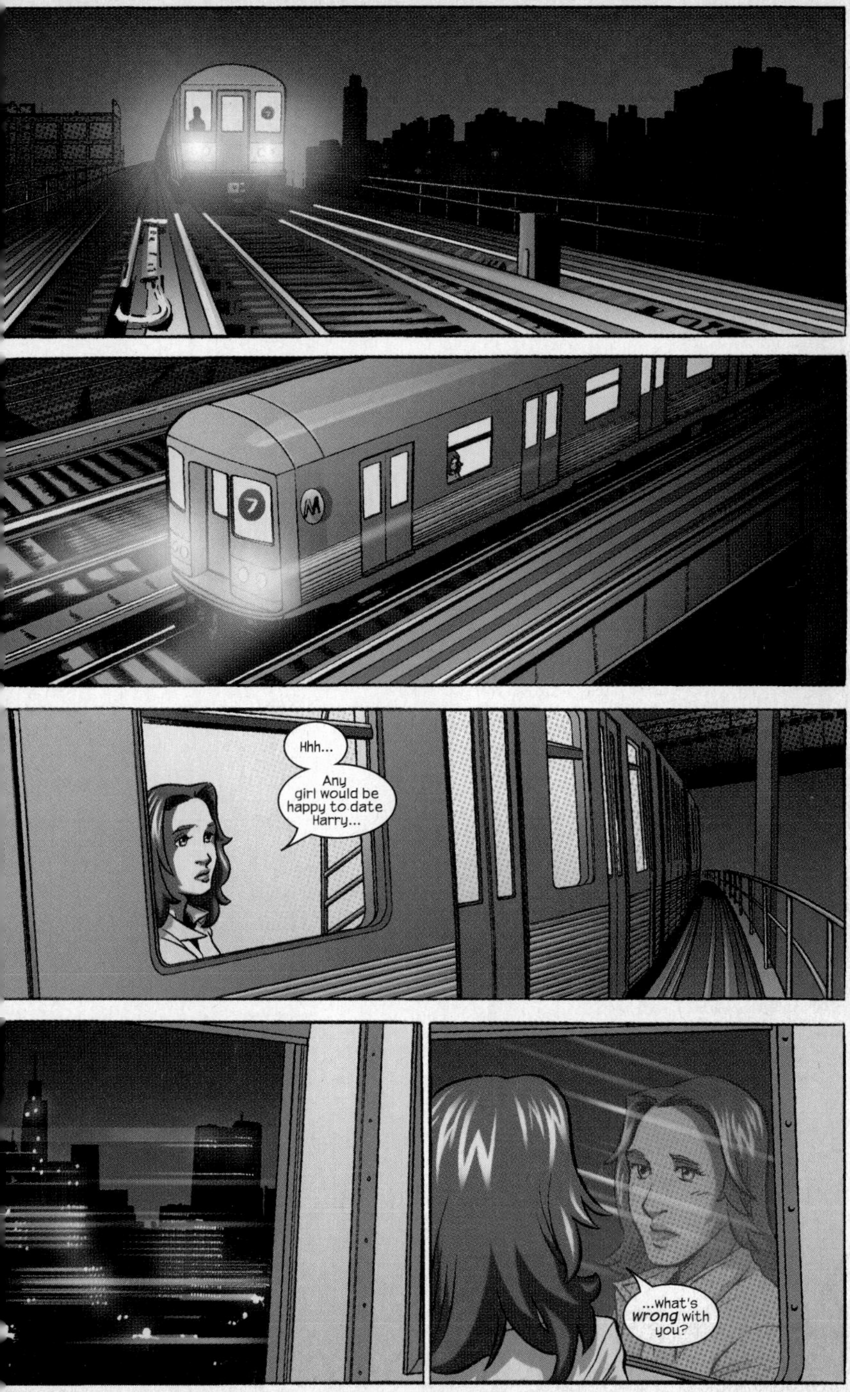
Hhh...
Any girl would be happy to date Harry...
...what's *wrong* with you?

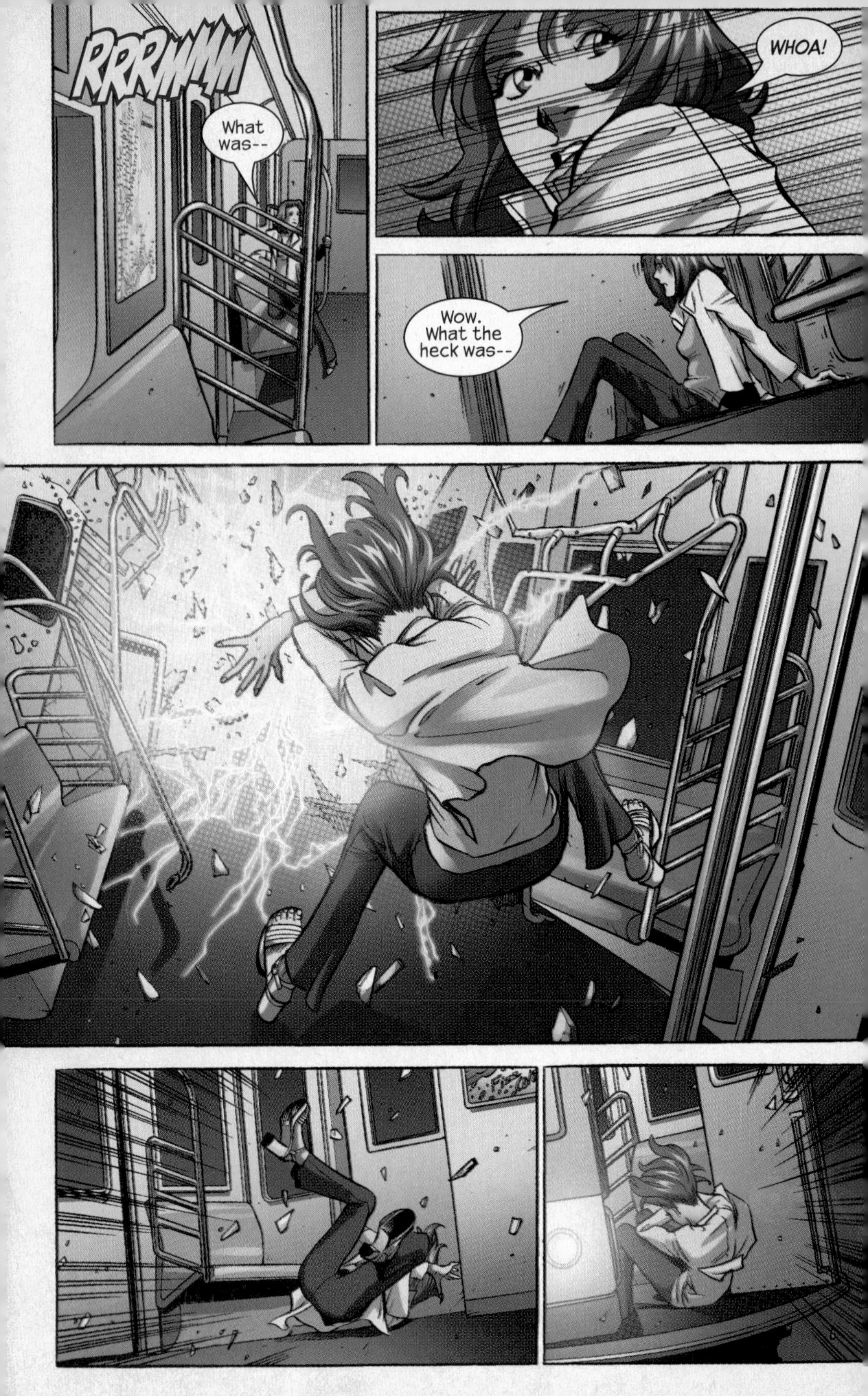
RRRMMMM
What was--
WHOA!
Wow. What the heck was--

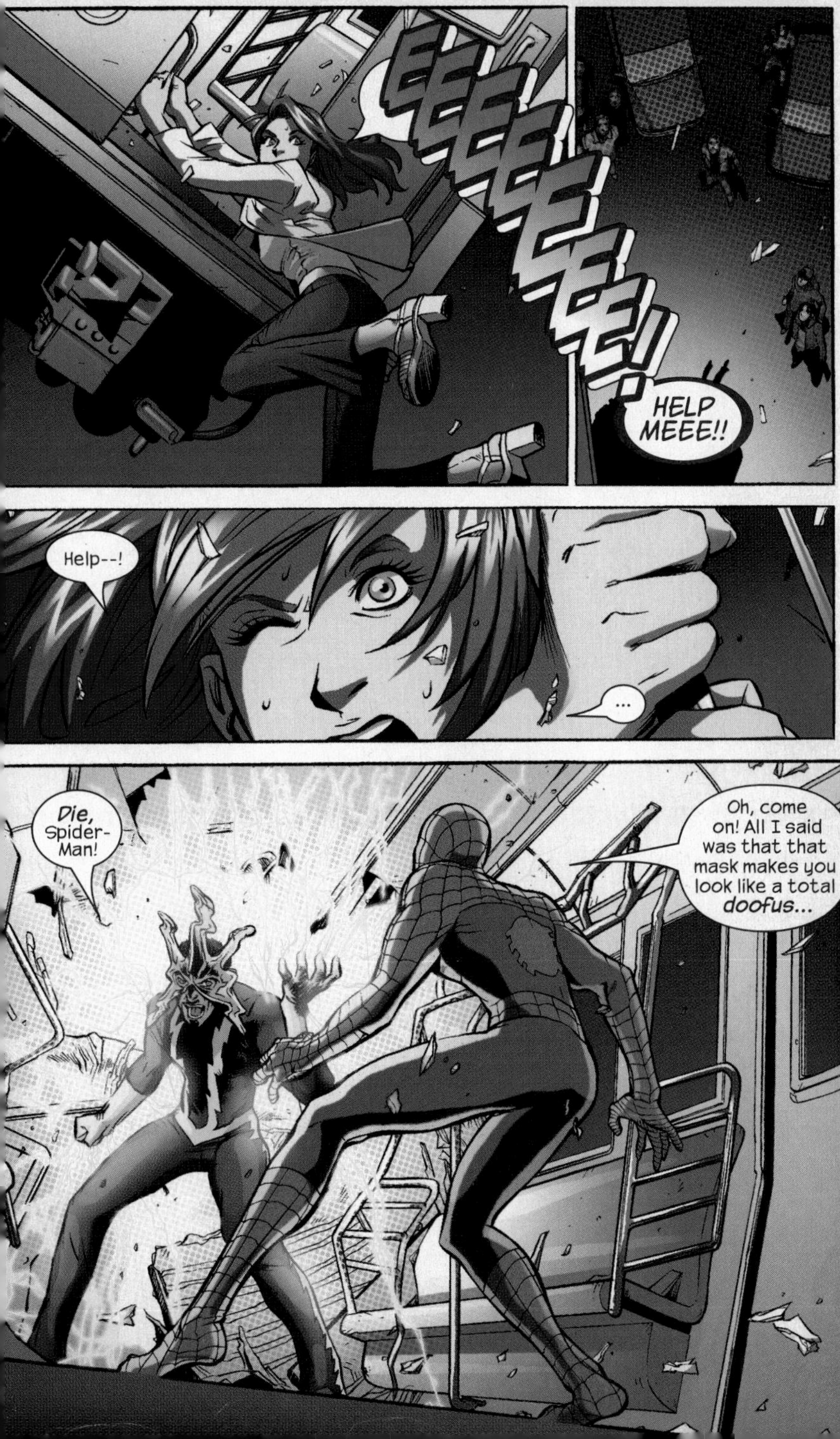
EEEEEEEEE!
HELP MEEE!!
Help--!
...
Die, Spider-Man!
Oh, come on! All I said was that that mask makes you look like a total doofus...

C'mon, *Electro*...I mean, yeah, sure, *all* us super-types like to hide our identities--

--but aren't you gonna at least *try* to look cool?

Shut up!

Make me!

AAA!!

HNNH!

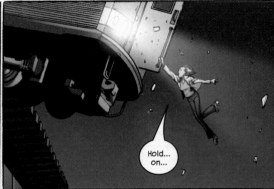

Hold... on...

No...

NO!!

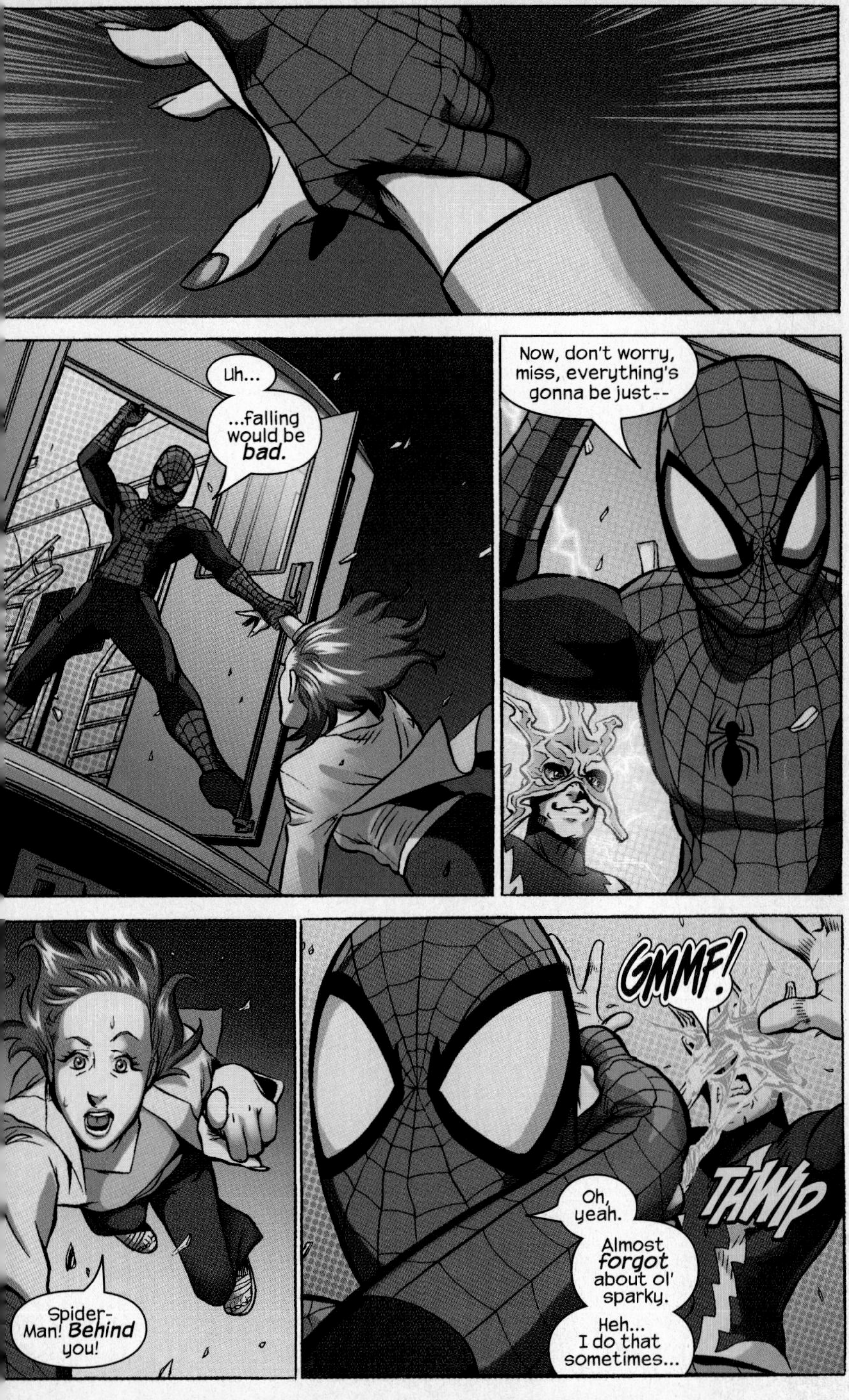

Uh...
...falling would be *bad.*
Now, don't worry, miss, everything's gonna be just--
Spider-Man! *Behind* you!
GMMF!
THWP
Oh, yeah.
Almost *forgot* about ol' sparky.
Heh... I do that sometimes...

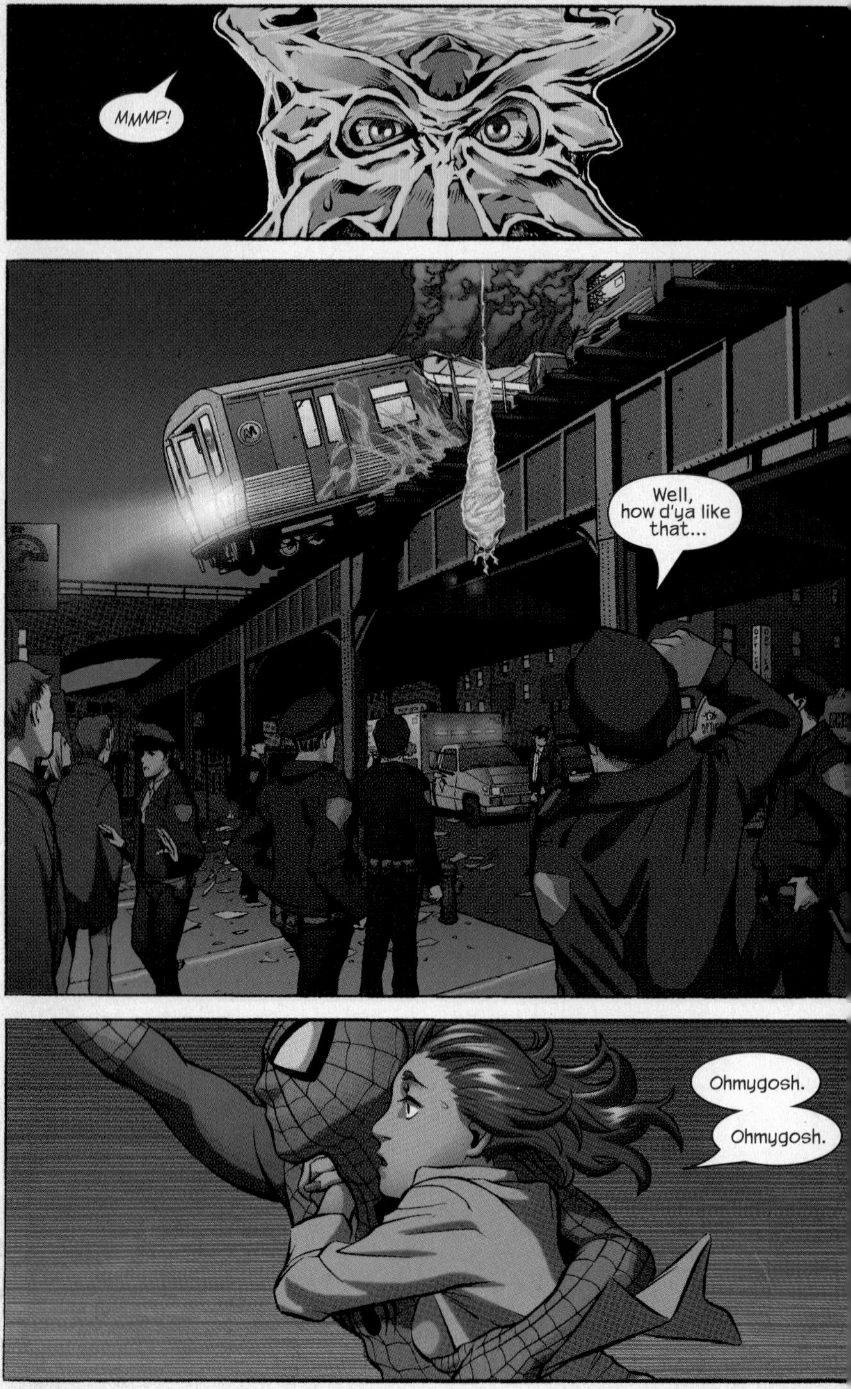
MMMP!
Well, how d'ya like that...
Ohmygosh.
Ohmygosh.

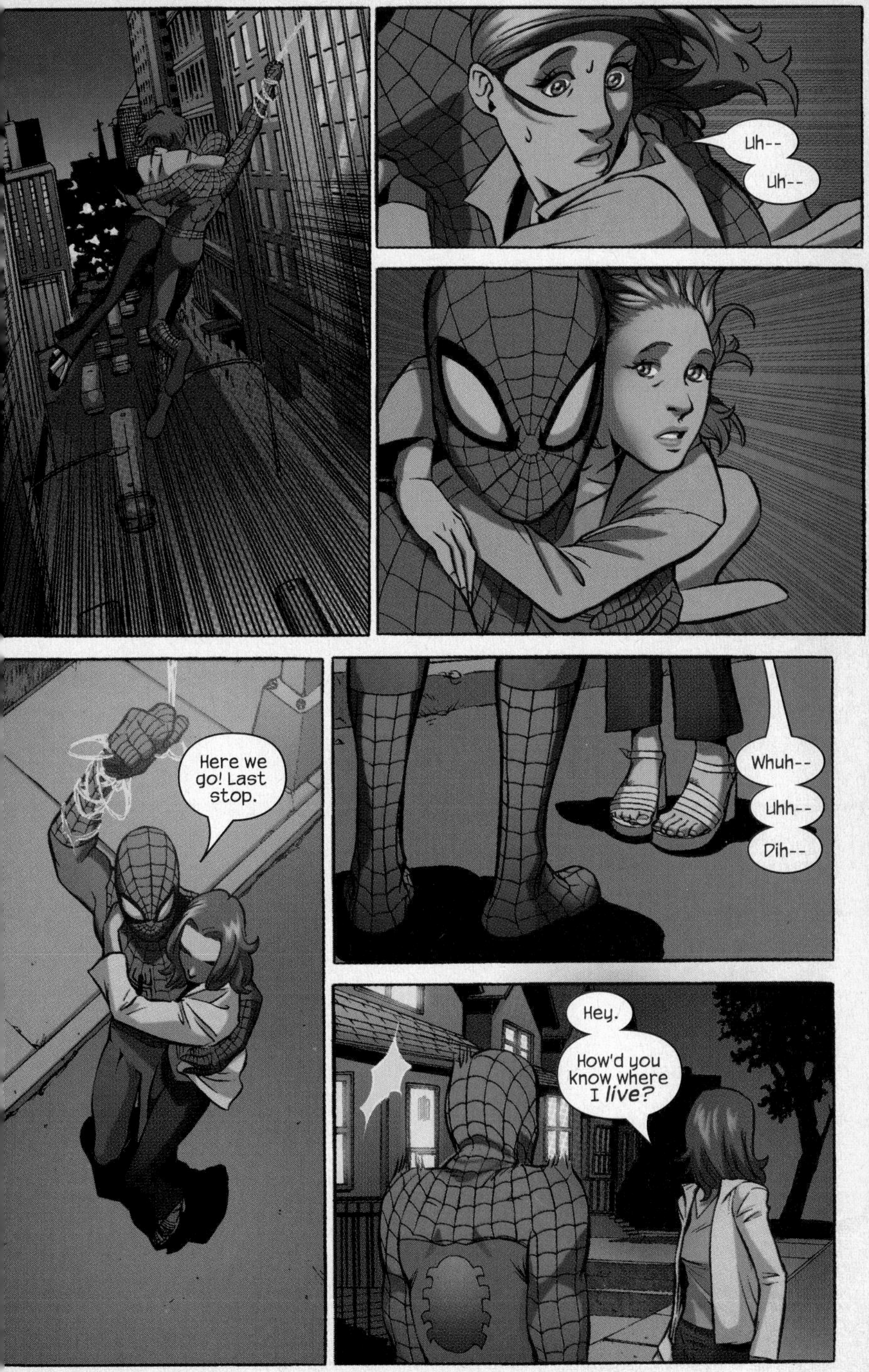
Uh--
Uh--
Here we go! Last stop.
Whuh--
Uhh--
Dih--
Hey.
How'd you know where I live?

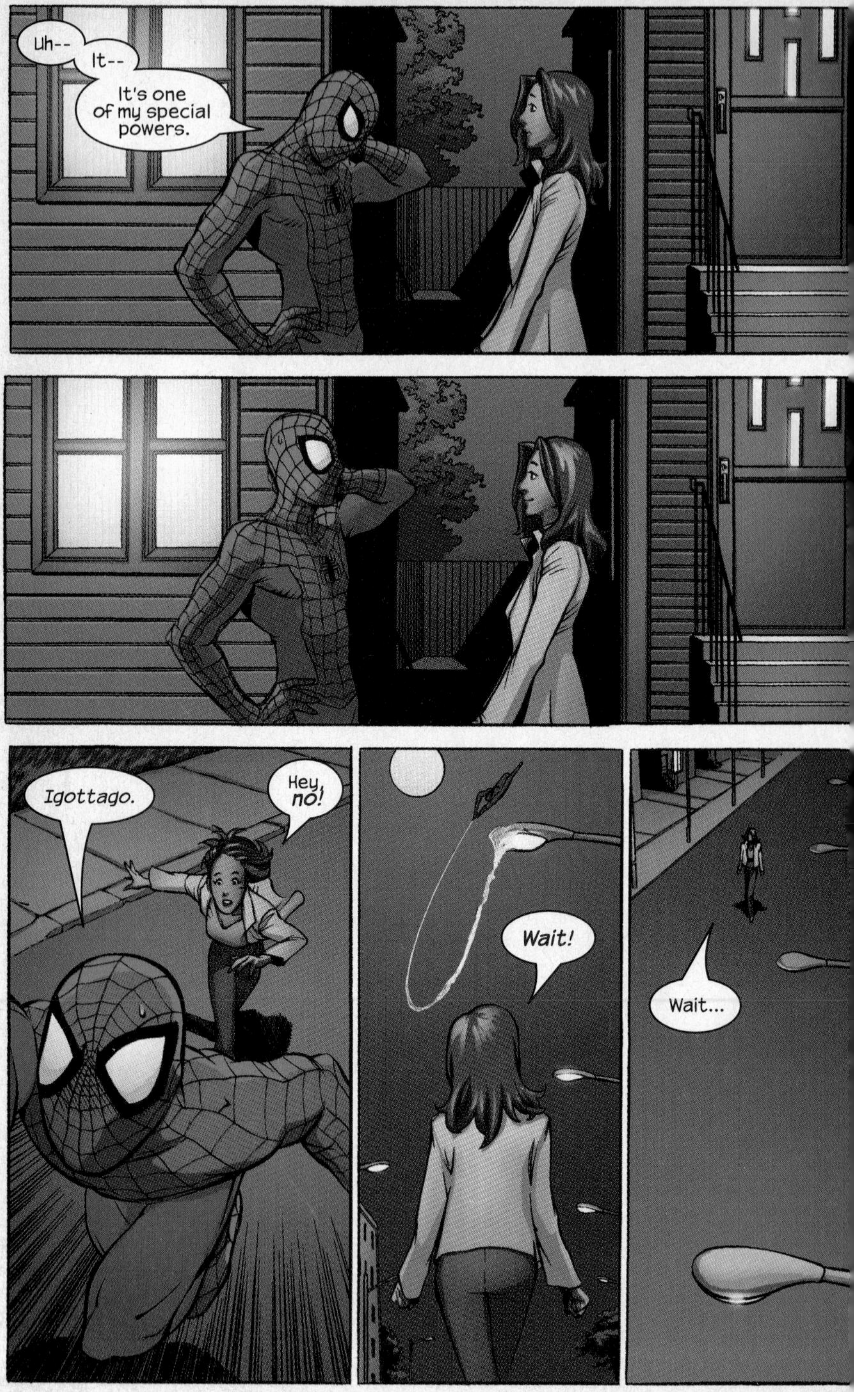
Uh--
It--
It's one of my special powers.
Igottago.
Hey, no!
Wait!
Wait...

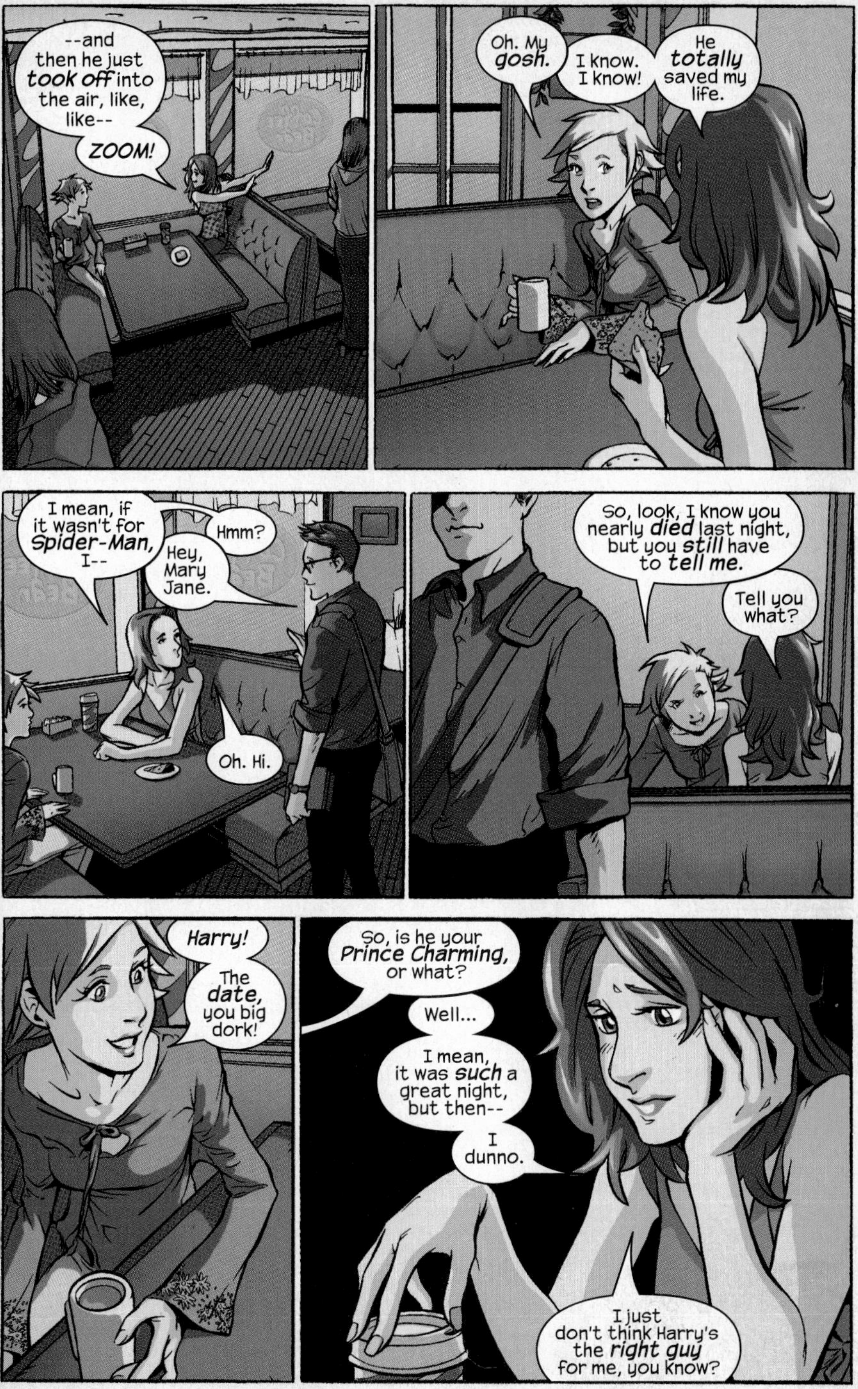
--and then he just took off into the air, like, like--
ZOOM!
Oh. My gosh.
I know. I know!
He totally saved my life.
I mean, if it wasn't for Spider-Man, I--
Hmm?
Hey, Mary Jane.
Oh. Hi.
So, look, I know you nearly died last night, but you still have to tell me.
Tell you what?
Harry!
The date, you big dork!
So, is he your Prince Charming, or what?
Well...
I mean, it was such a great night, but then--
I dunno.
I just don't think Harry's the right guy for me, you know?

Great. So now we're back to where we *started*, and you have no one to go to the Homecoming dance with.

Well, actually, I kinda have an *idea* about that.

But you're gonna think I'm *crazy*...

I already *do*, so just *spill* it!

Okay, here goes...

I want *Spider-Man* to be my Homecoming date.

THE REAL THING

Sean McKeever — Writer | Takeshi Miyazawa — Pencils | Norman Lee — Inks | Christina Strain — Colors | VC's Randy Gentile & Dave Sharpe — Letters | MacKenzie Cadenhead — Editor | C.B. Cebulski — Consulting Editor | Joe Quesada — chief | Dan Buckley — Publisher

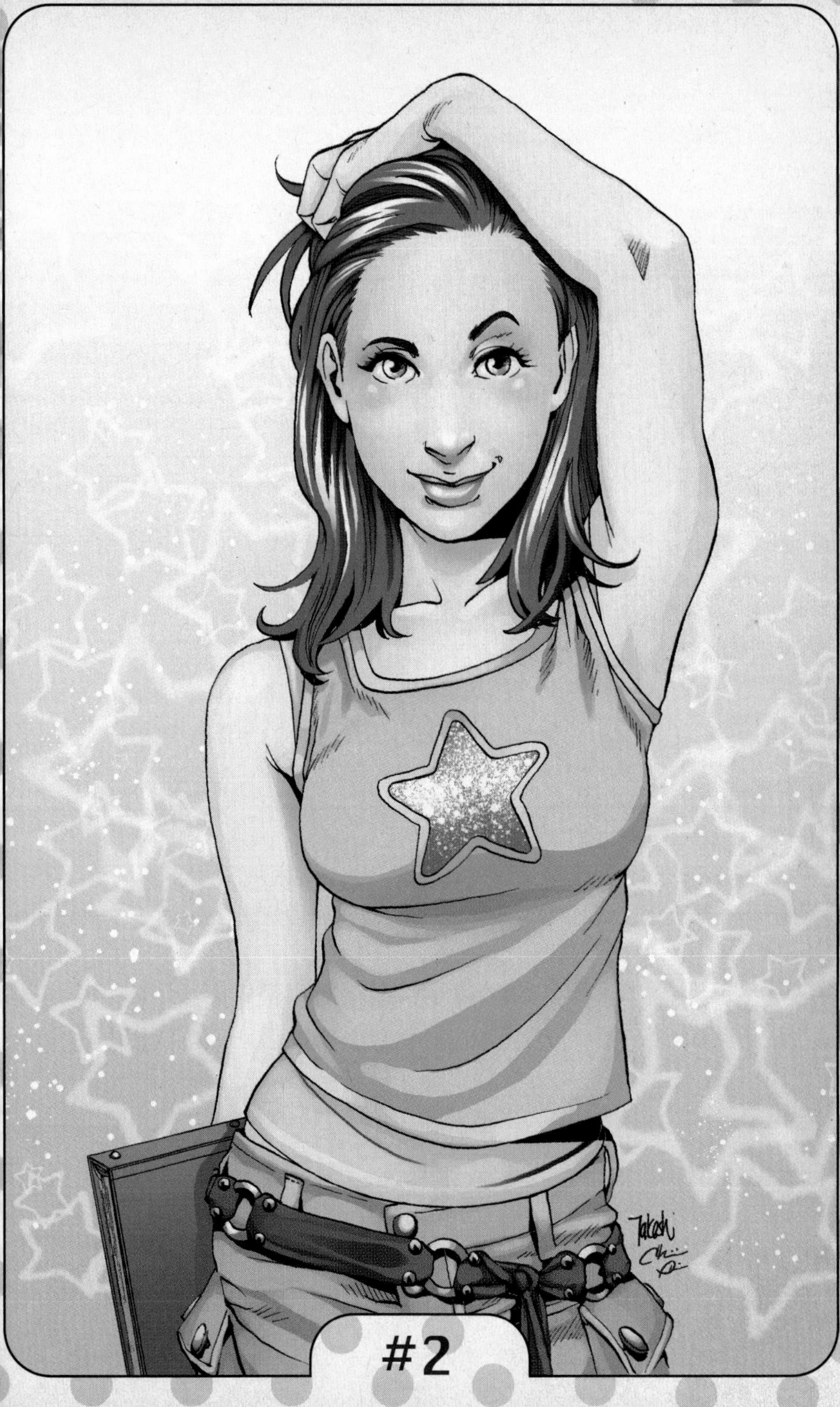

#2

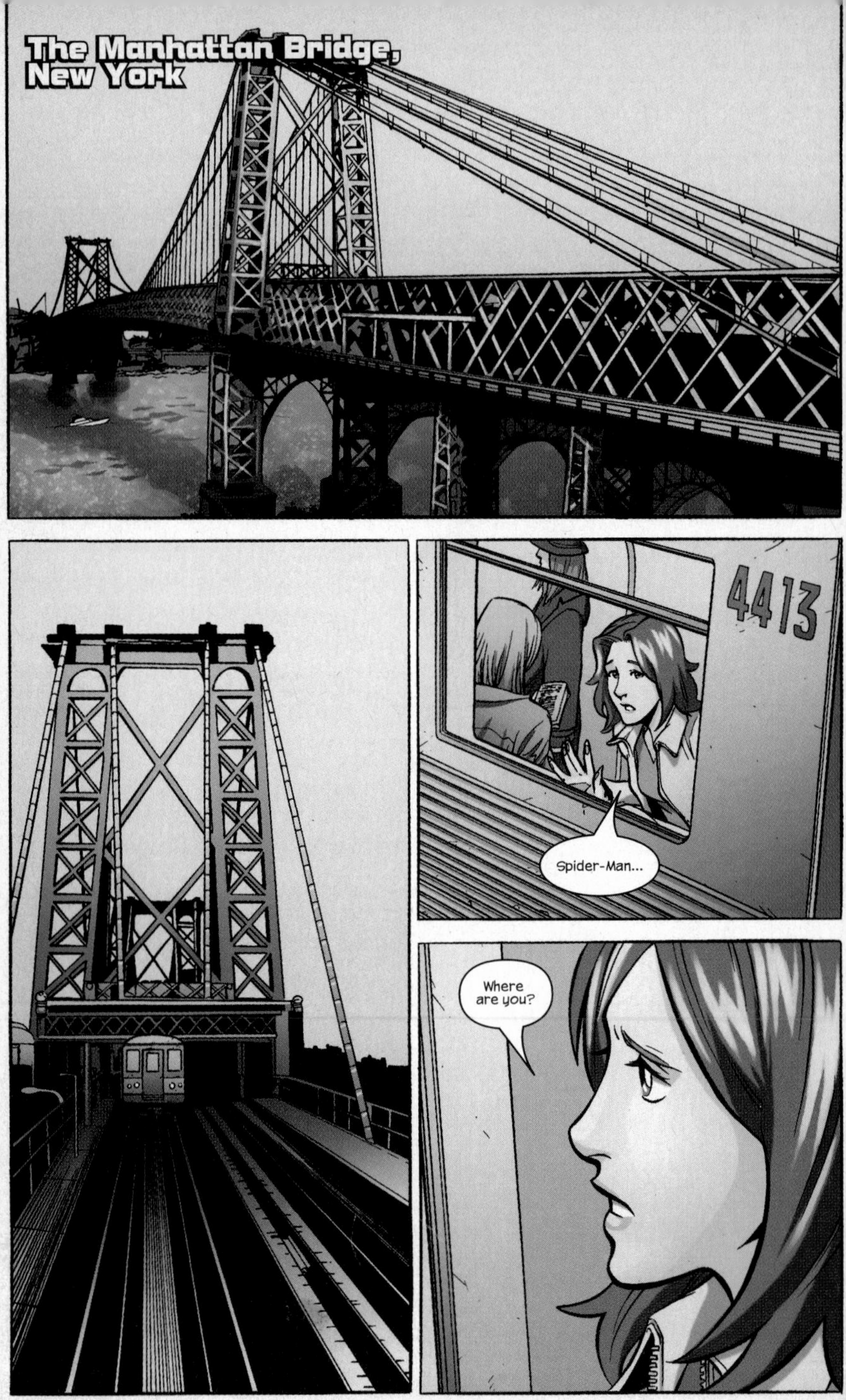
The Manhattan Bridge, New York
4413
Spider-Man...
Where are you?

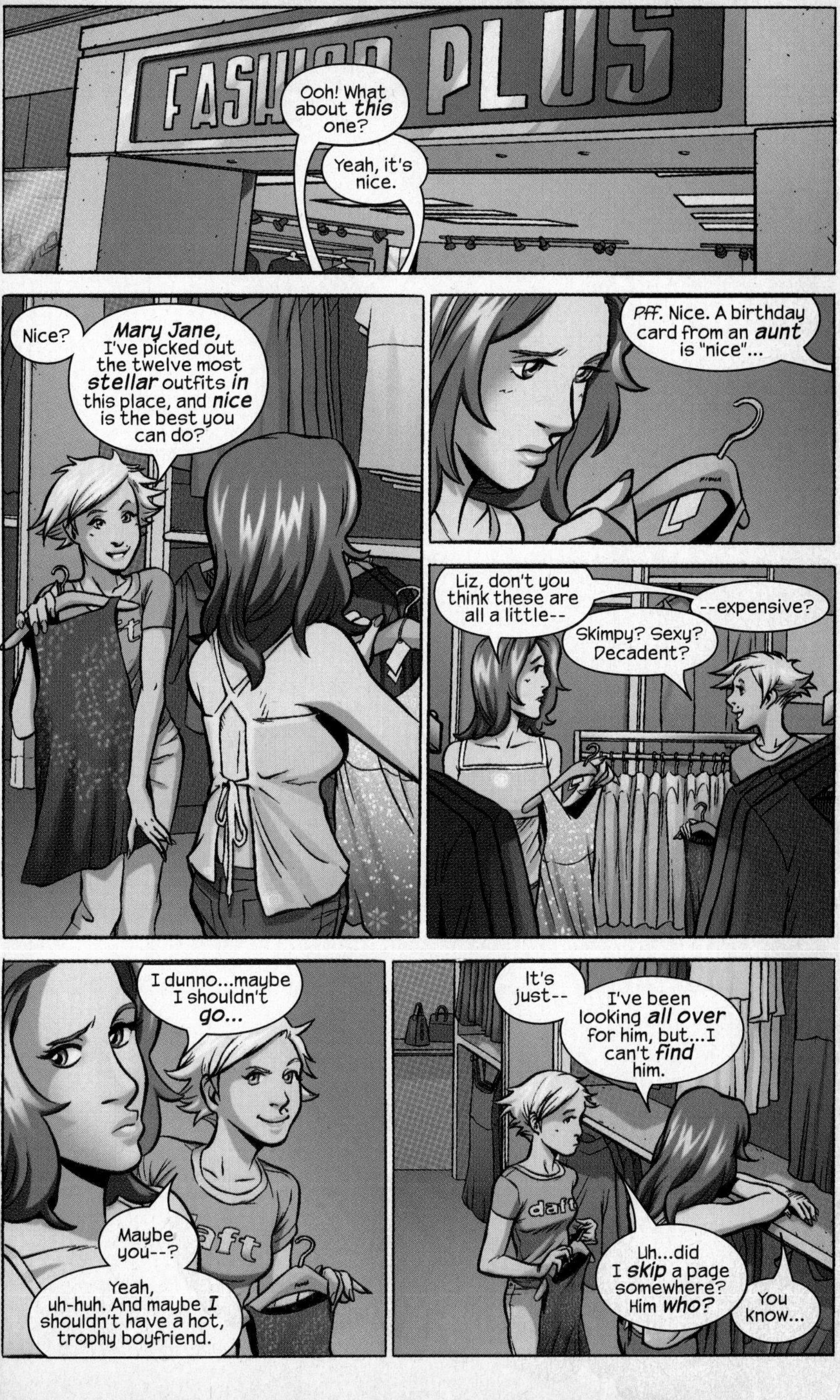
FASHION PLUS
Ooh! What about this one?
Yeah, it's nice.
Nice?
Mary Jane, I've picked out the twelve most stellar outfits in this place, and nice is the best you can do?
Pff. Nice. A birthday card from an aunt is "nice"...
Liz, don't you think these are all a little--
--expensive?
Skimpy? Sexy? Decadent?
I dunno...maybe I shouldn't go...
Maybe you--?
Yeah, uh-huh. And maybe I shouldn't have a hot, trophy boyfriend.
It's just--
I've been looking all over for him, but...I can't find him.
Uh...did I skip a page somewhere? Him who?
You know...

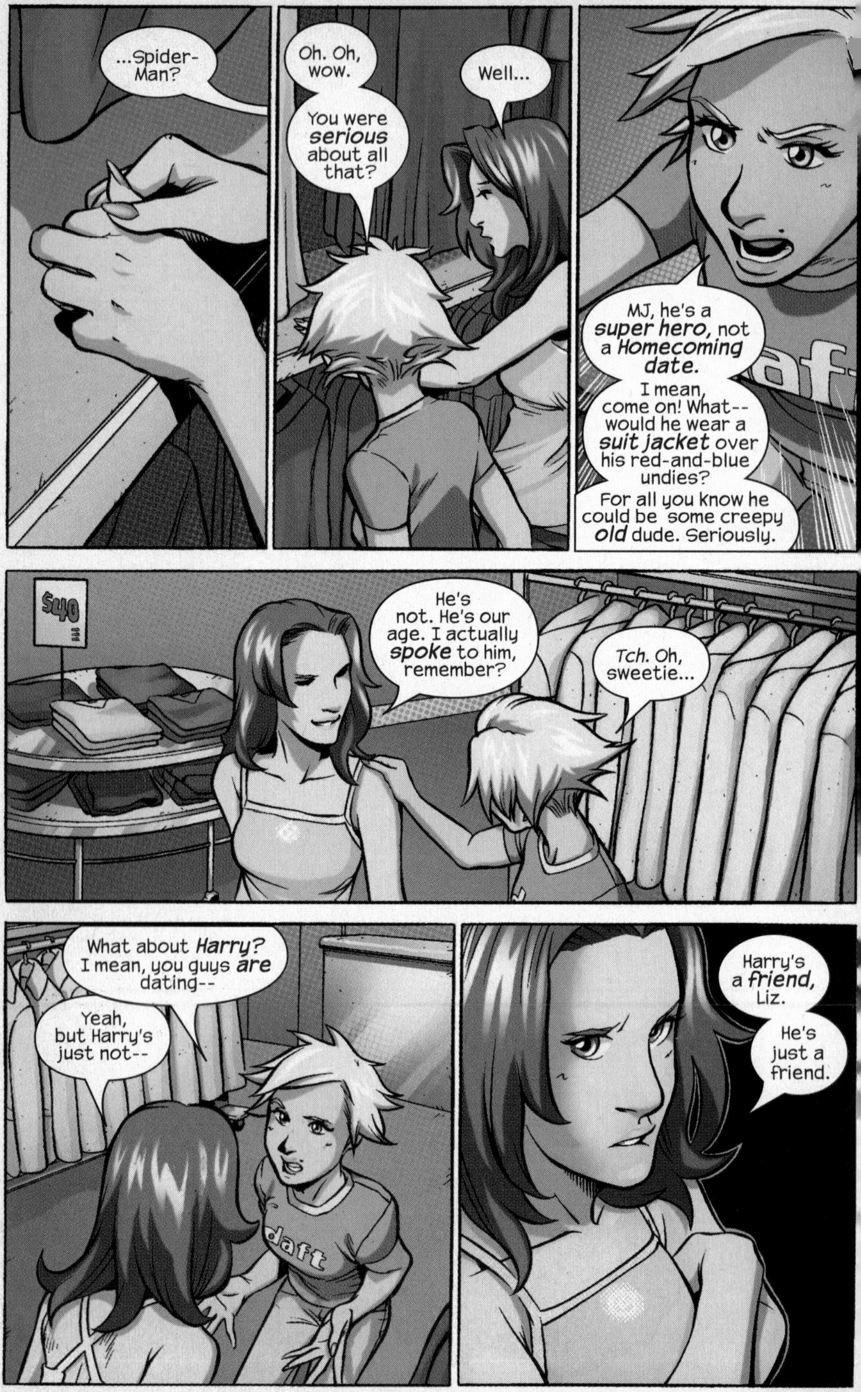
...Spider-Man?
Oh. Oh, wow.
You were serious about all that?
Well...
MJ, he's a super hero, not a Homecoming date.
I mean, come on! What--would he wear a suit jacket over his red-and-blue undies?
For all you know he could be some creepy old dude. Seriously.
$40
He's not. He's our age. I actually spoke to him, remember?
Tch. Oh, sweetie...
What about Harry? I mean, you guys are dating--
Yeah, but Harry's just not--
daft
Harry's a friend, Liz.
He's just a friend.

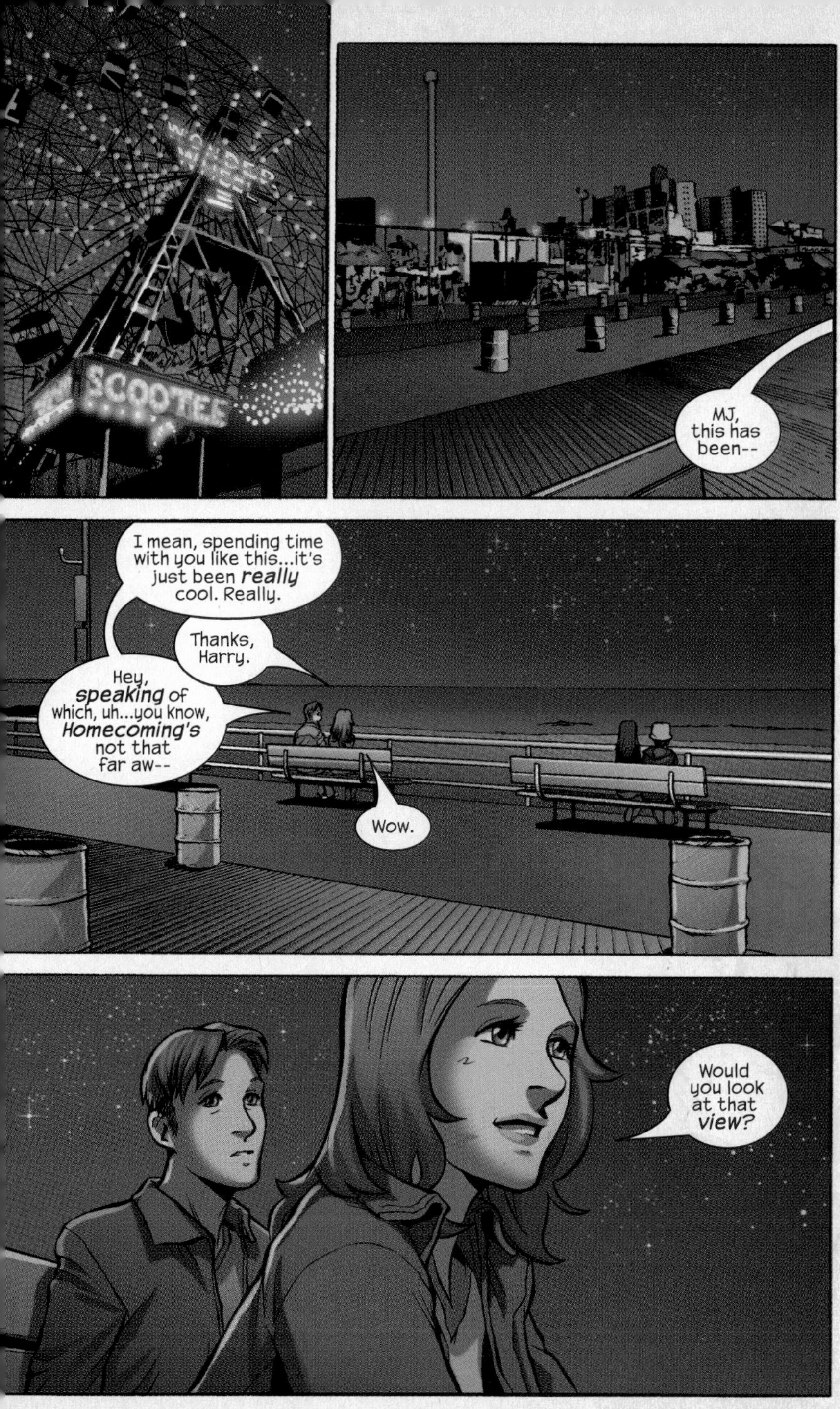
WONDER WHEEL
SCOOTER
MJ, this has been--
I mean, spending time with you like this...it's just been *really* cool. Really.
Thanks, Harry.
Hey, *speaking* of which, uh...you know, *Homecoming's* not that far aw--
Wow.
Would you look at that *view?*

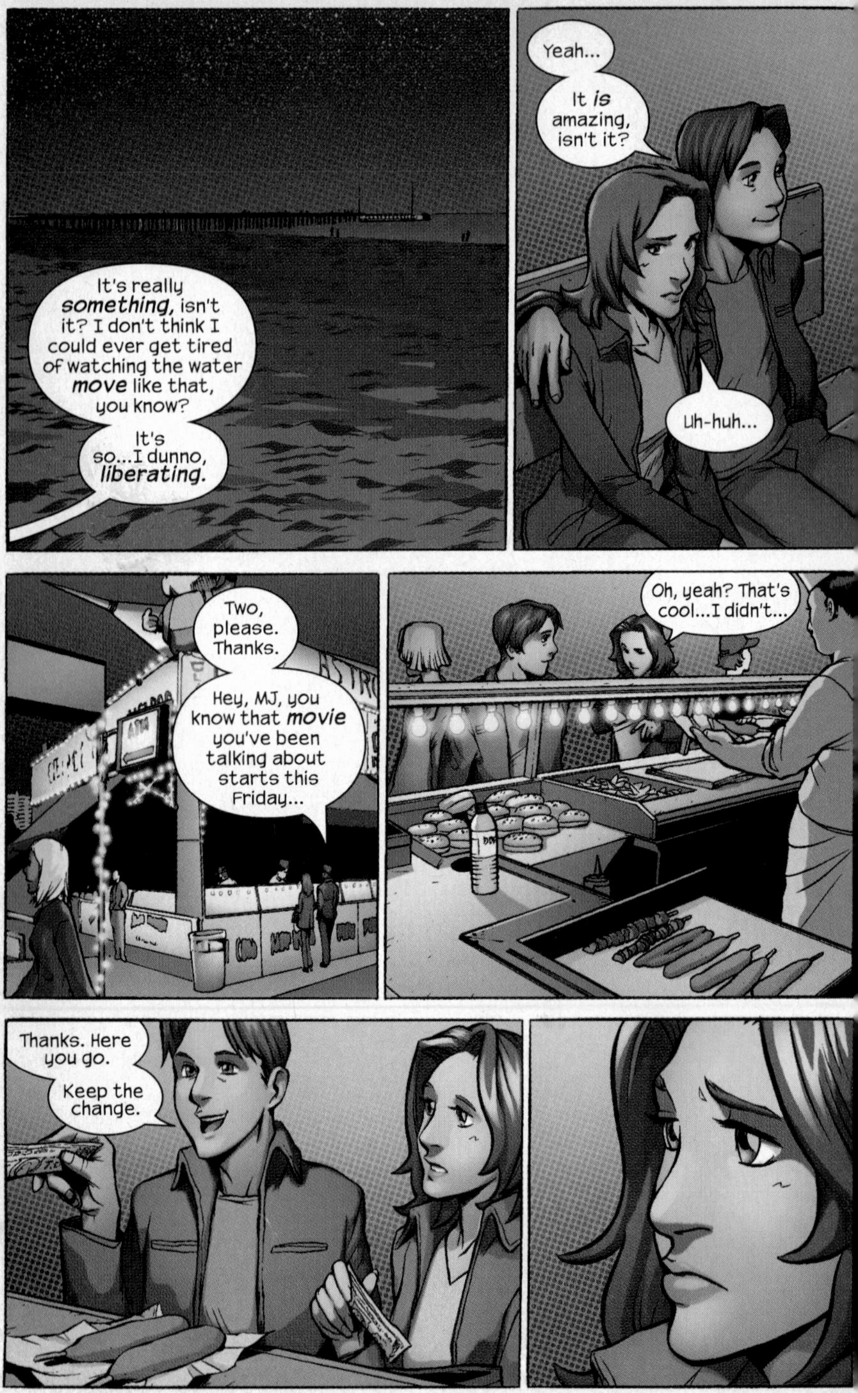
It's really *something,* isn't it? I don't think I could ever get tired of watching the water *move* like that, you know?
It's so...I dunno, *liberating.*
Yeah...
It *is* amazing, isn't it?
Uh-huh...
Two, please. Thanks.
Hey, MJ, you know that *movie* you've been talking about starts this Friday...
Oh, yeah? That's cool...I didn't...
Thanks. Here you go.
Keep the change.

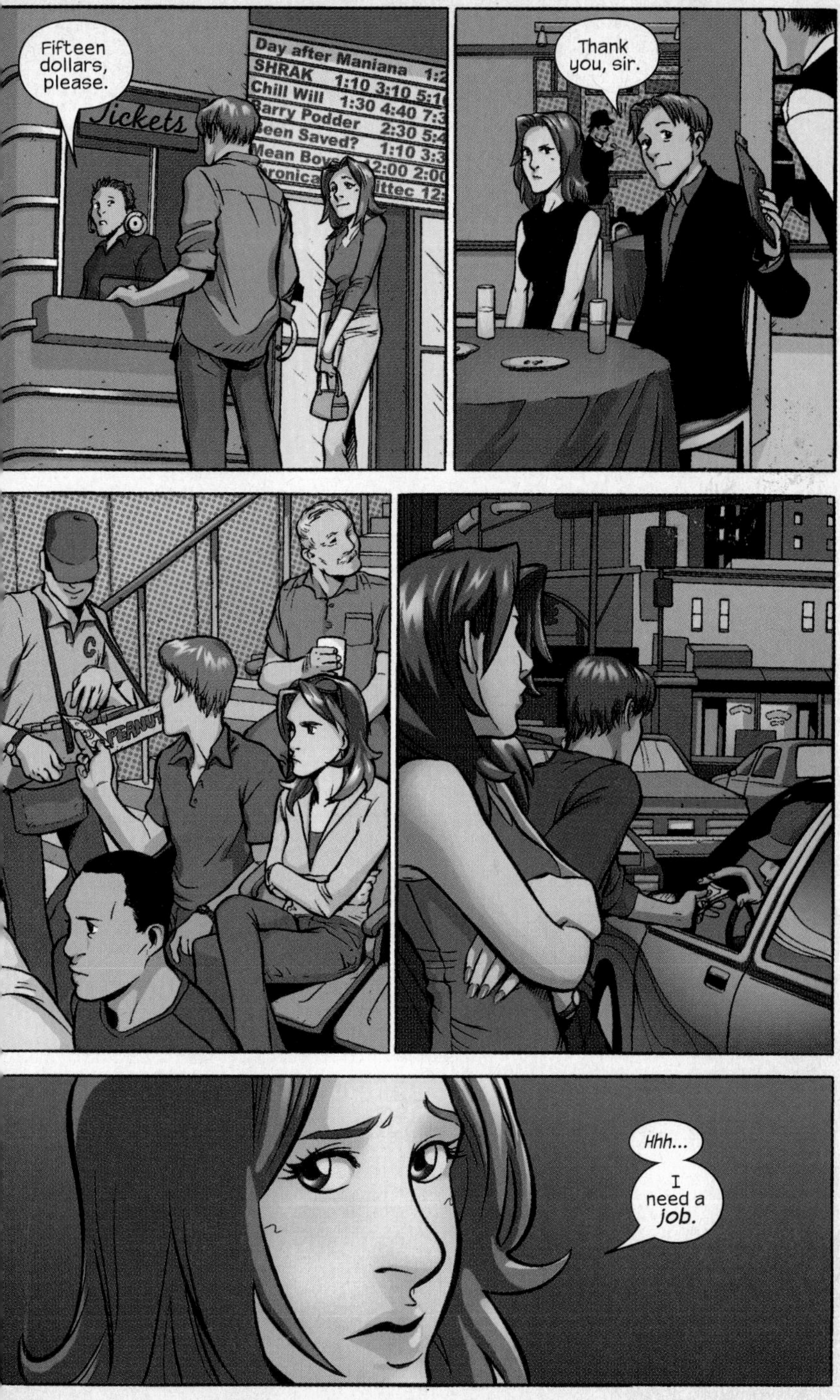
Fifteen dollars, please.
Tickets
Day after Maniana 1:2
SHRAK 1:10 3:10 5:1
Chill Will 1:30 4:40 7:3
Barry Podder 2:30 5:4
Been Saved? 1:10 3:3
Mean Boys 12:00 2:00
Thank you, sir.
PEANUT
Hhh...
I need a job.

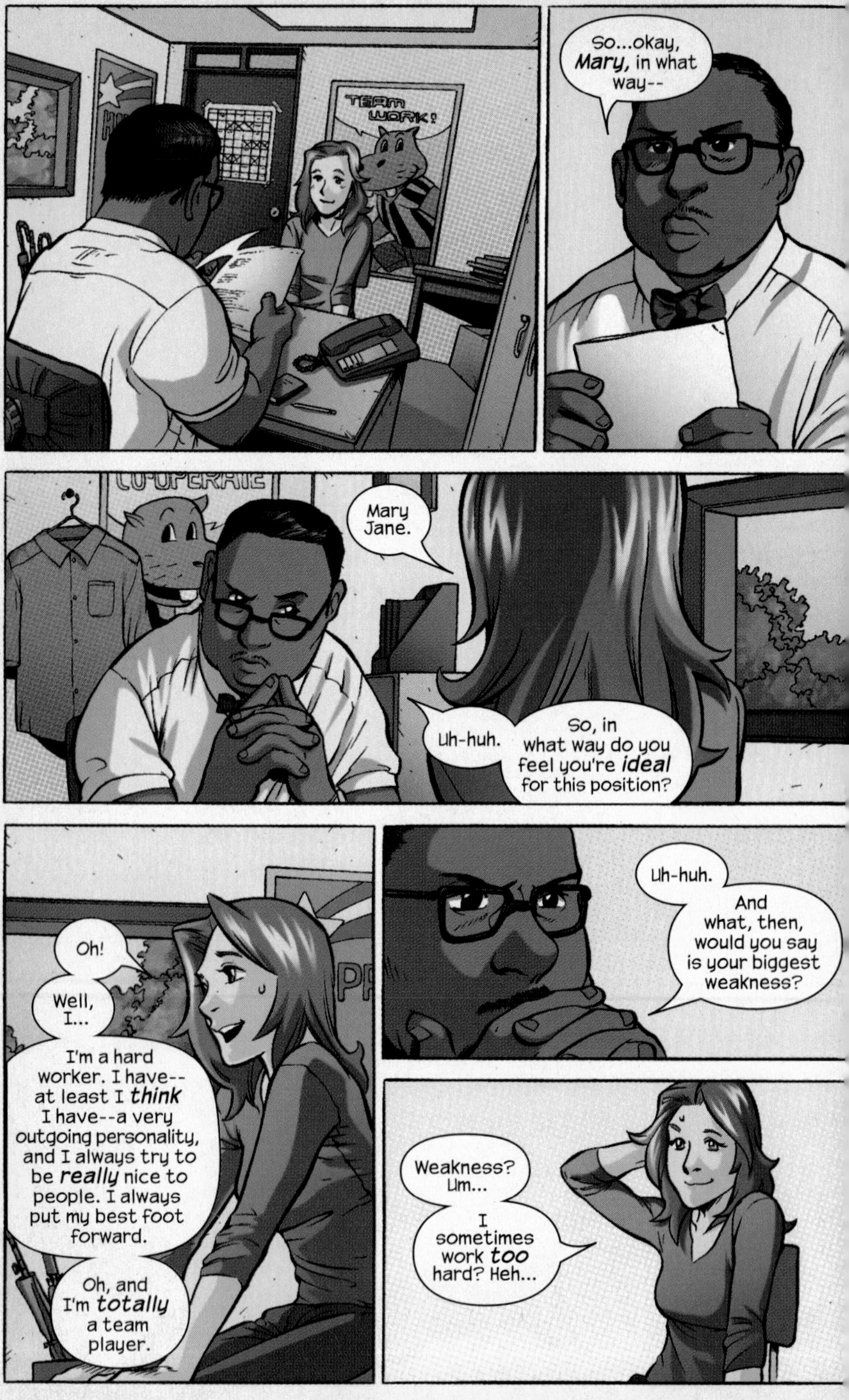
TEAM WORK!
So...okay, Mary, in what way--
CO-OPERATE
Mary Jane.
Uh-huh.
So, in what way do you feel you're ideal for this position?
Oh!
Well, I...
I'm a hard worker. I have--at least I think I have--a very outgoing personality, and I always try to be really nice to people. I always put my best foot forward.
Oh, and I'm totally a team player.
Uh-huh.
And what, then, would you say is your biggest weakness?
Weakness? Um...
I sometimes work too hard? Heh...

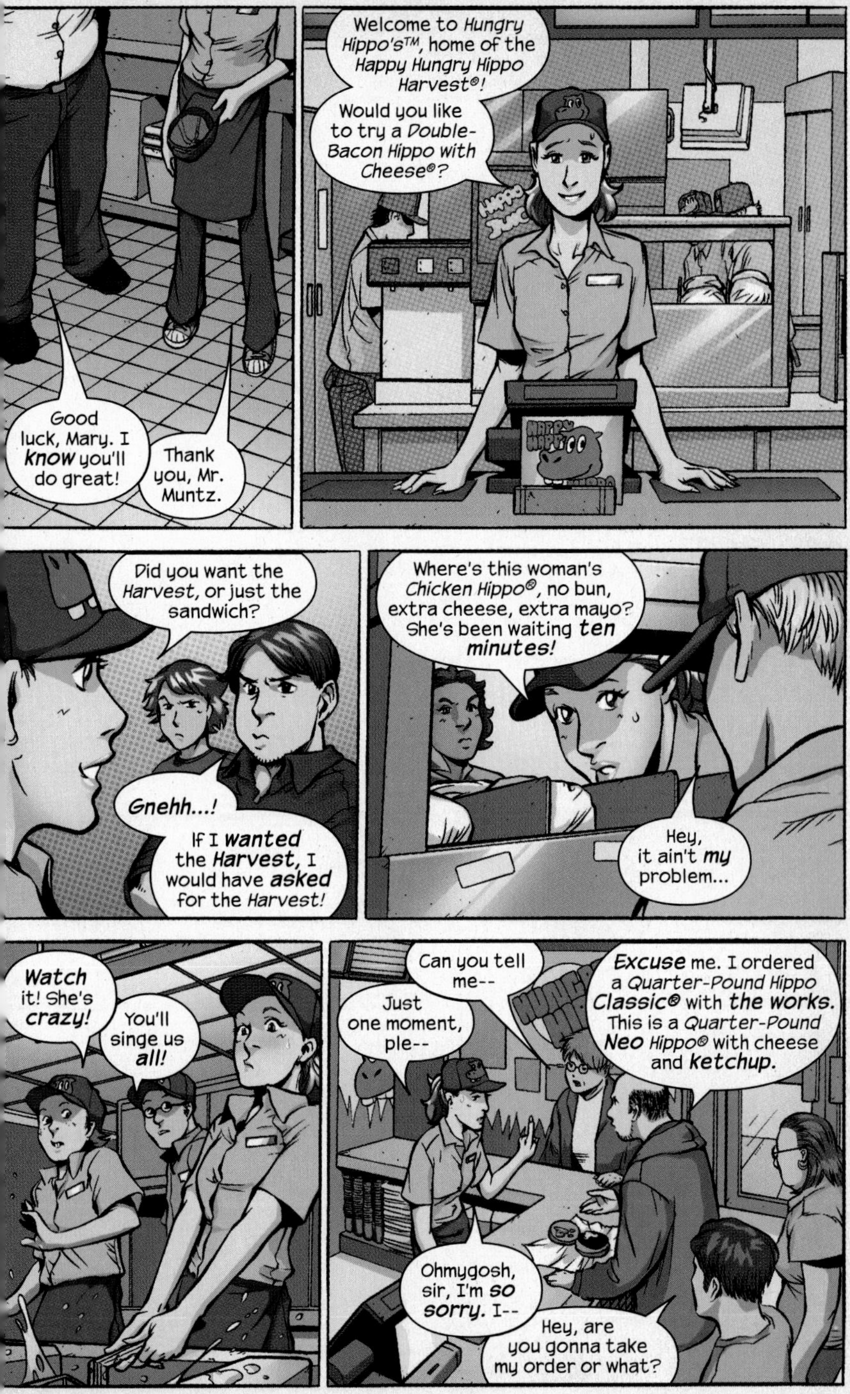
Good luck, Mary. I know you'll do great!
Thank you, Mr. Muntz.
Welcome to Hungry Hippo's™, home of the Happy Hungry Hippo Harvest®!
Would you like to try a Double-Bacon Hippo with Cheese®?
Did you want the Harvest, or just the sandwich?
Gnehh...!
If I wanted the Harvest, I would have asked for the Harvest!
Where's this woman's Chicken Hippo®, no bun, extra cheese, extra mayo? She's been waiting ten minutes!
Hey, it ain't my problem...
Watch it! She's crazy!
You'll singe us all!
Can you tell me--
Excuse me. I ordered a Quarter-Pound Hippo Classic® with the works. This is a Quarter-Pound Neo Hippo® with cheese and ketchup.
Just one moment, ple--
Ohmygosh, sir, I'm so sorry. I--
Hey, are you gonna take my order or what?

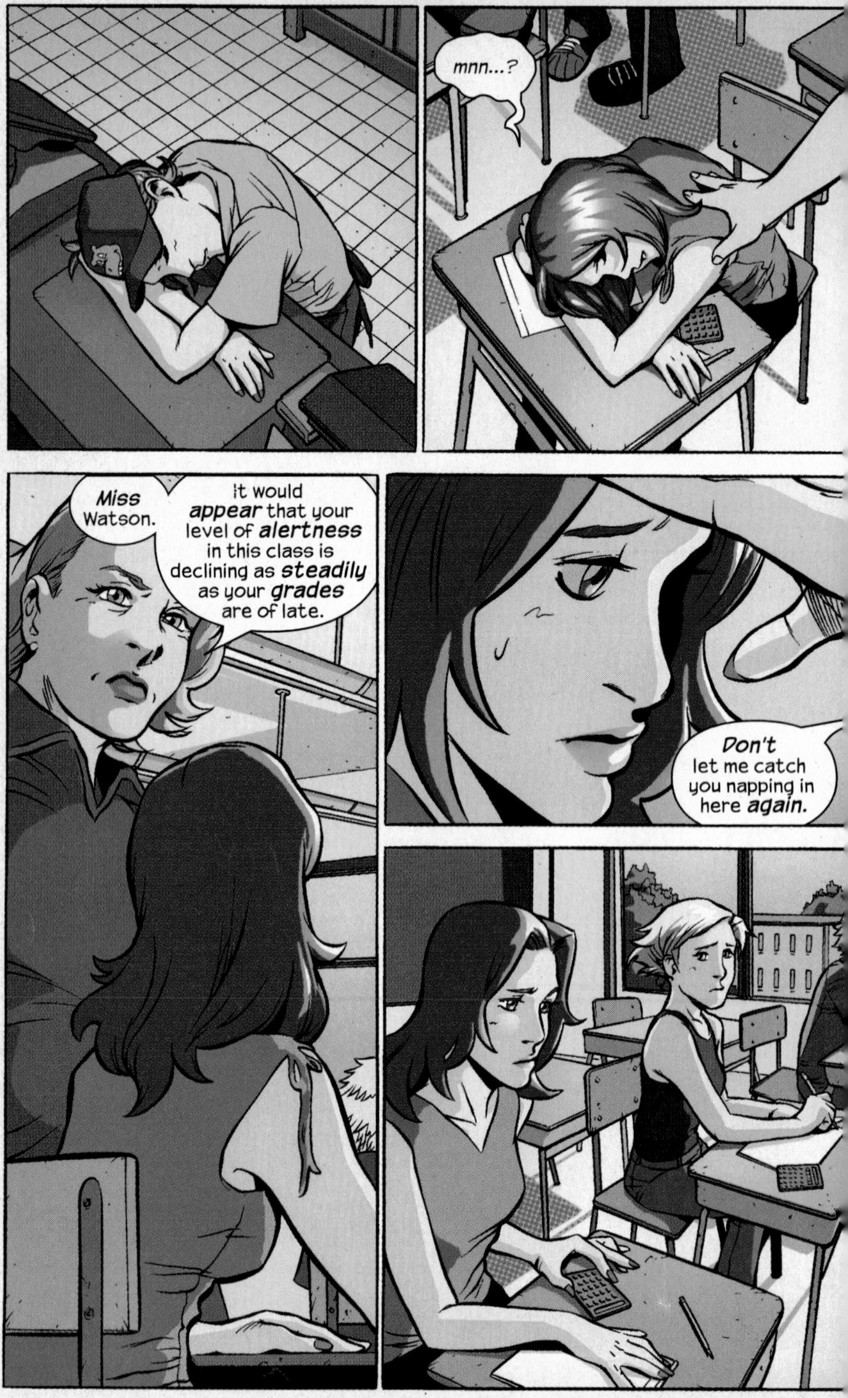
mnn...?
Miss Watson.
It would appear that your level of alertness in this class is declining as steadily as your grades are of late.
Don't let me catch you napping in here again.

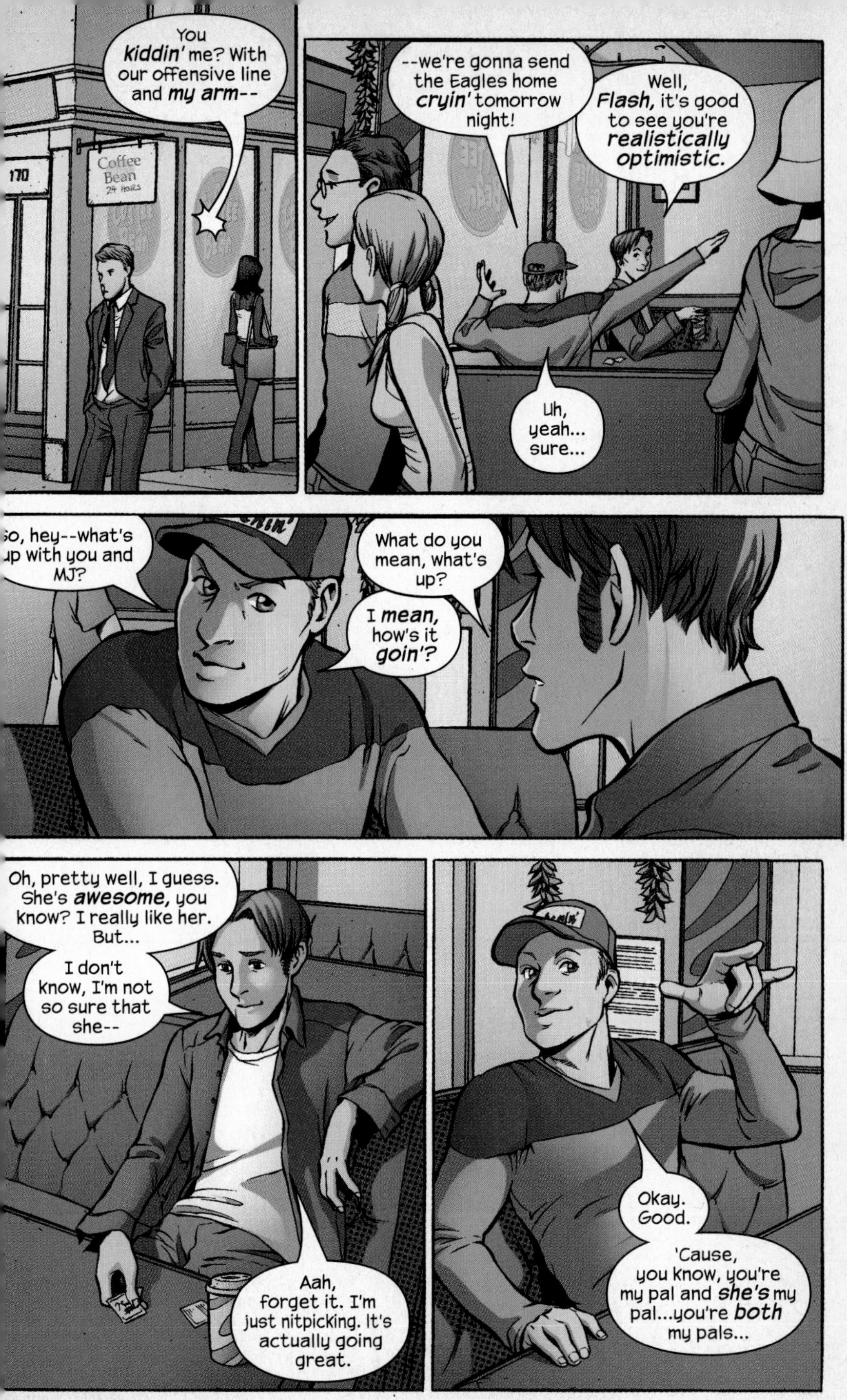
You kiddin' me? With our offensive line and my arm--
Coffee Bean 24 Hours
170
--we're gonna send the Eagles home cryin' tomorrow night!
Well, Flash, it's good to see you're realistically optimistic.
Uh, yeah... sure...
So, hey--what's up with you and MJ?
What do you mean, what's up?
I mean, how's it goin'?
Oh, pretty well, I guess. She's awesome, you know? I really like her. But...
I don't know, I'm not so sure that she--
Aah, forget it. I'm just nitpicking. It's actually going great.
Okay. Good.
'Cause, you know, you're my pal and she's my pal...you're both my pals...

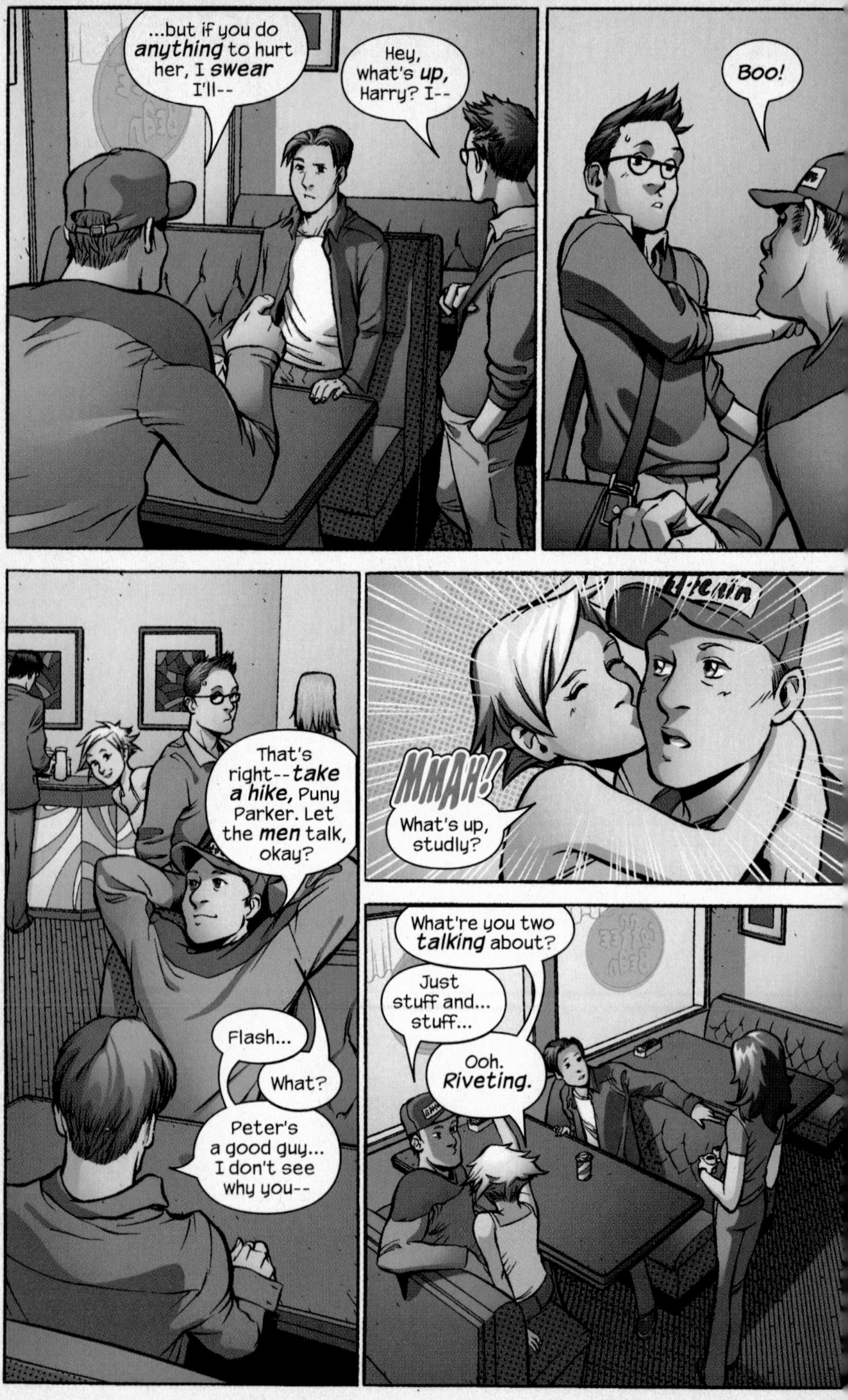

...but if you do *anything* to hurt her, I *swear* I'll--
Hey, what's up, Harry? I--
Boo!
That's right--*take a hike,* Puny Parker. Let the *men* talk, okay?
Flash...
What?
Peter's a good guy... I don't see why you--
MMAH!
What's up, studly?
What're you two *talking* about?
Just stuff and... stuff...
Ooh. *Riveting.*

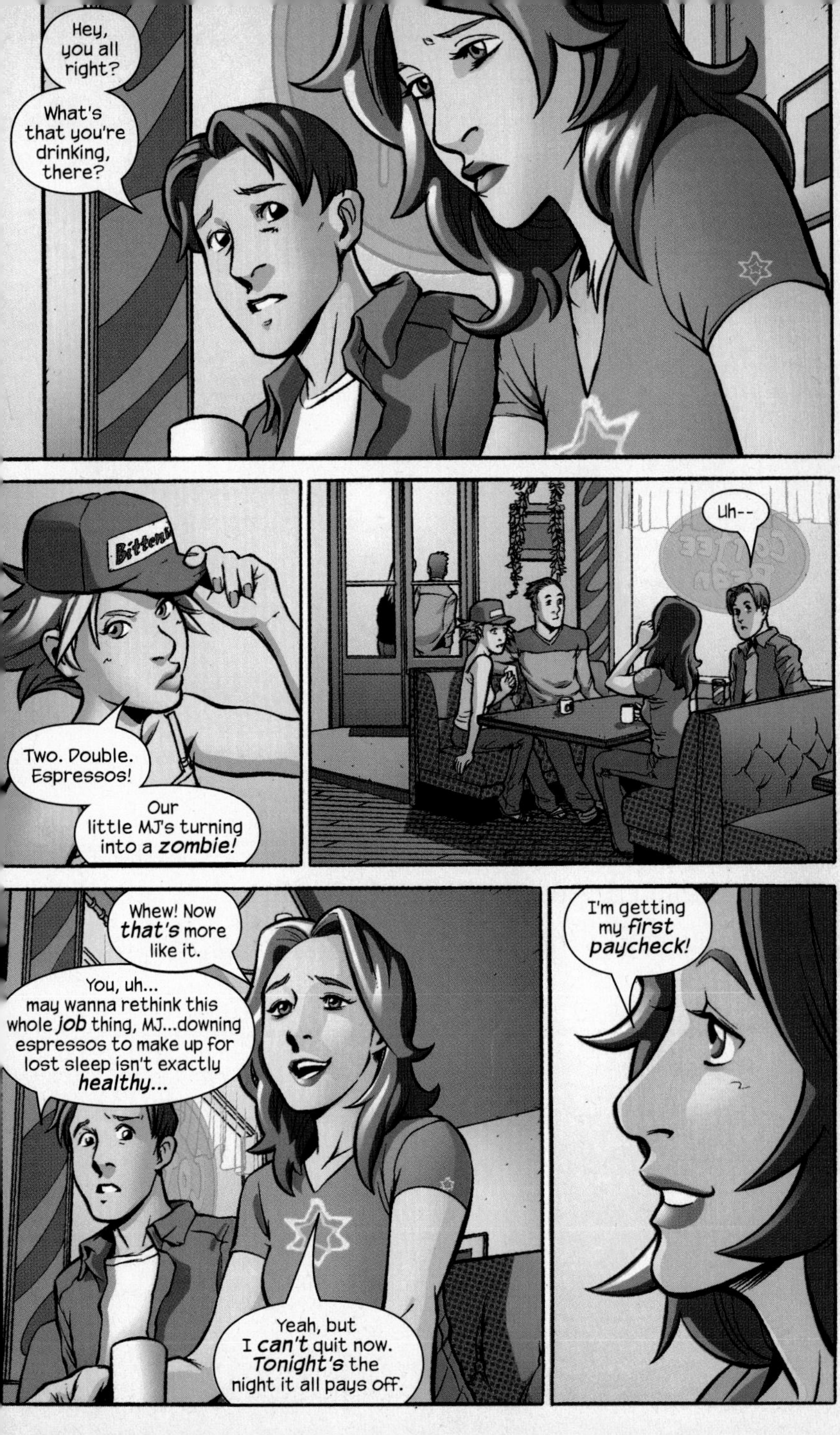
Hey, you all right?
What's that you're drinking, there?
Two. Double. Espressos!
Our little MJ's turning into a *zombie!*
Uh--
Whew! Now *that's* more like it.
You, uh... may wanna rethink this whole *job* thing, MJ...downing espressos to make up for lost sleep isn't exactly *healthy...*
Yeah, but I *can't* quit now. *Tonight's* the night it all pays off.
I'm getting my *first paycheck!*

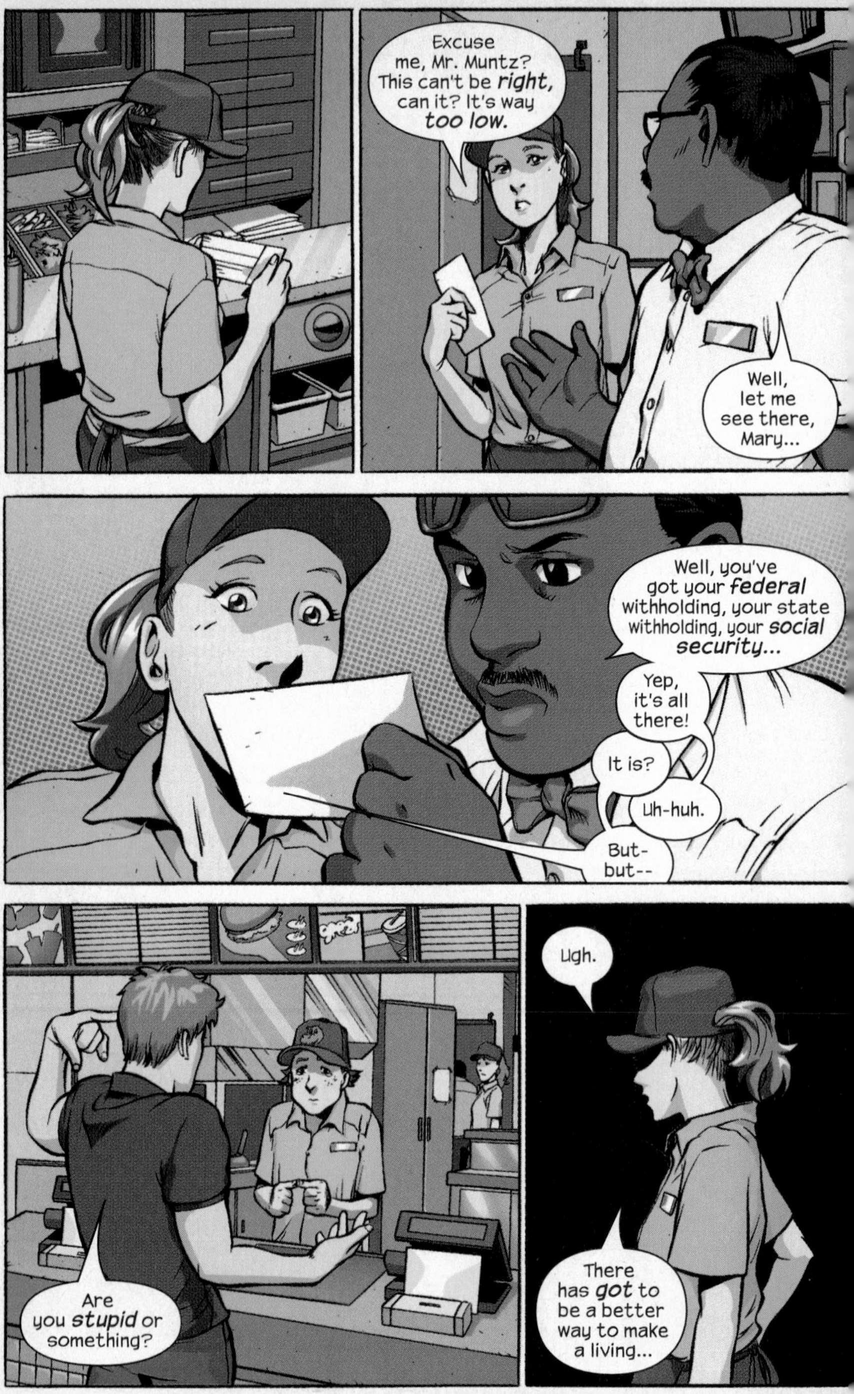

Excuse me, Mr. Muntz? This can't be *right,* can it? It's way *too low.*
Well, let me see there, Mary...
Well, you've got your *federal* withholding, your state withholding, your *social security...*
Yep, it's all there!
It is?
Uh-huh.
But-but--
Are you *stupid* or something?
Ugh.
There has *got* to be a better way to make a living...

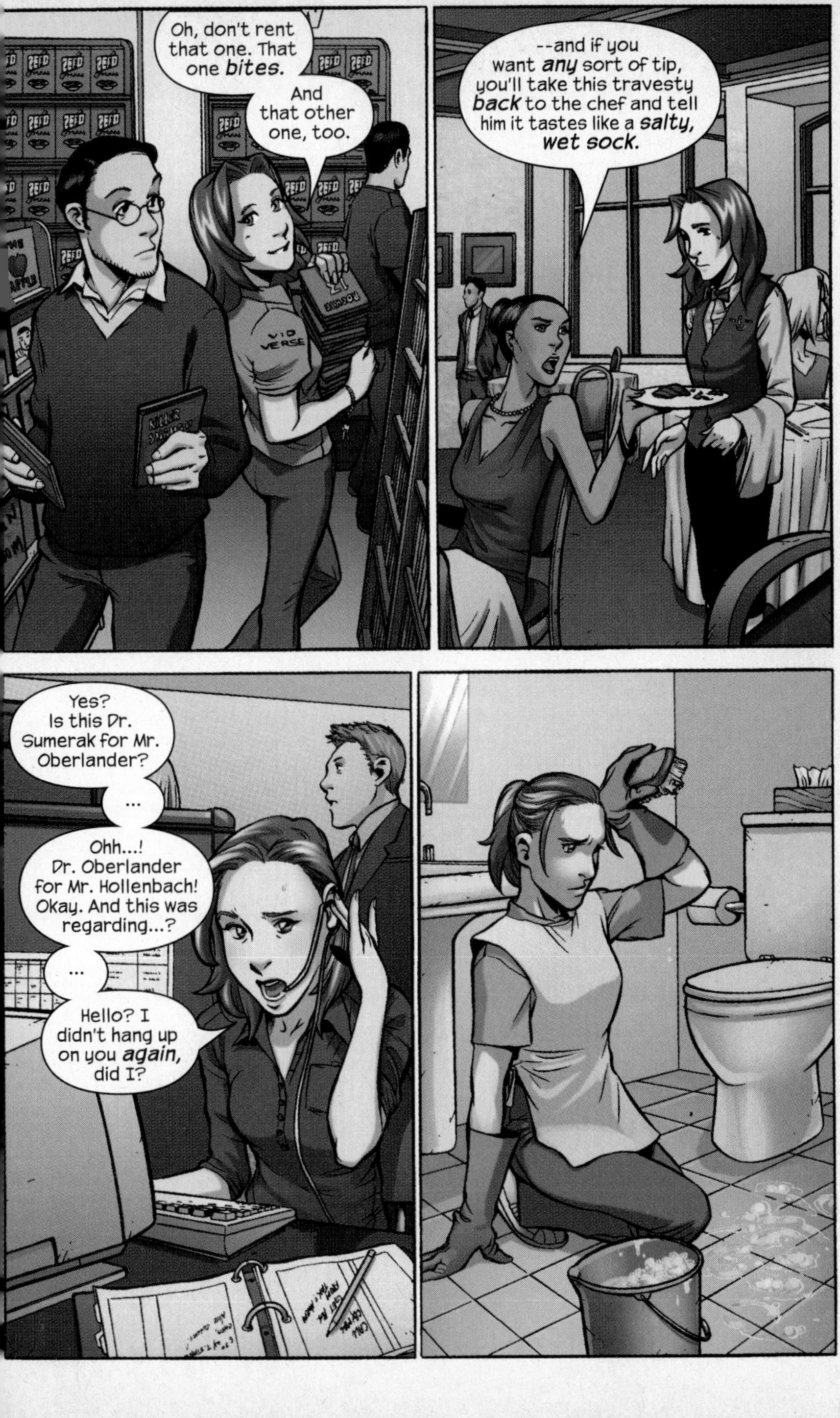
Oh, don't rent that one. That one *bites.*
And that other one, too.
VID VERSE
--and if you want *any* sort of tip, you'll take this travesty *back* to the chef and tell him it tastes like a *salty, wet sock.*
Yes? Is this Dr. Sumerak for Mr. Oberlander?
...
Ohh...! Dr. Oberlander for Mr. Hollenbach! Okay. And this was regarding...?
...
Hello? I didn't hang up on you *again,* did I?

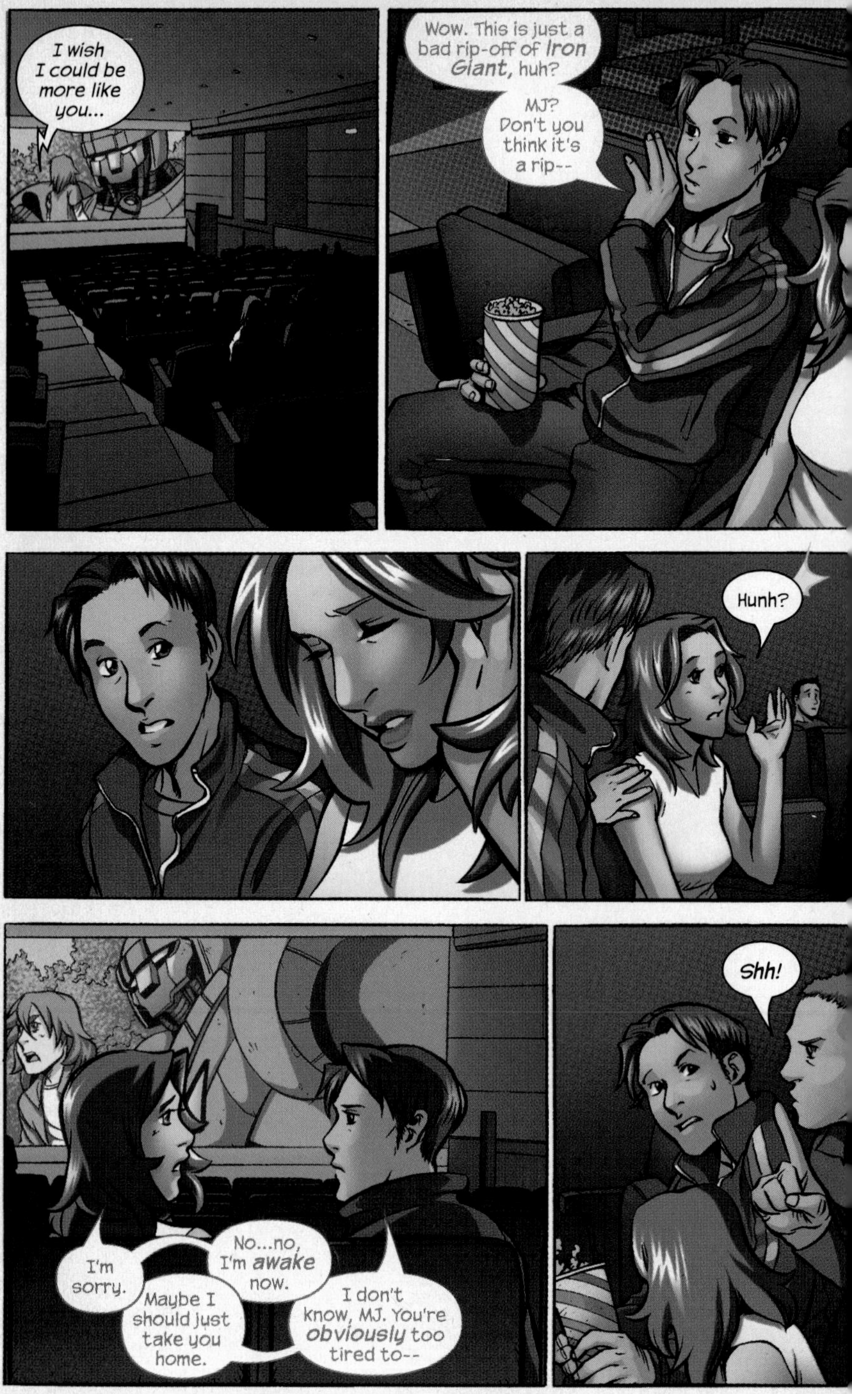

I wish I could be more like you...
Wow. This is just a bad rip-off of Iron Giant, huh?
MJ? Don't you think it's a rip--
Hunh?
I'm sorry.
No...no, I'm awake now.
Maybe I should just take you home.
I don't know, MJ. You're obviously too tired to--
Shh!

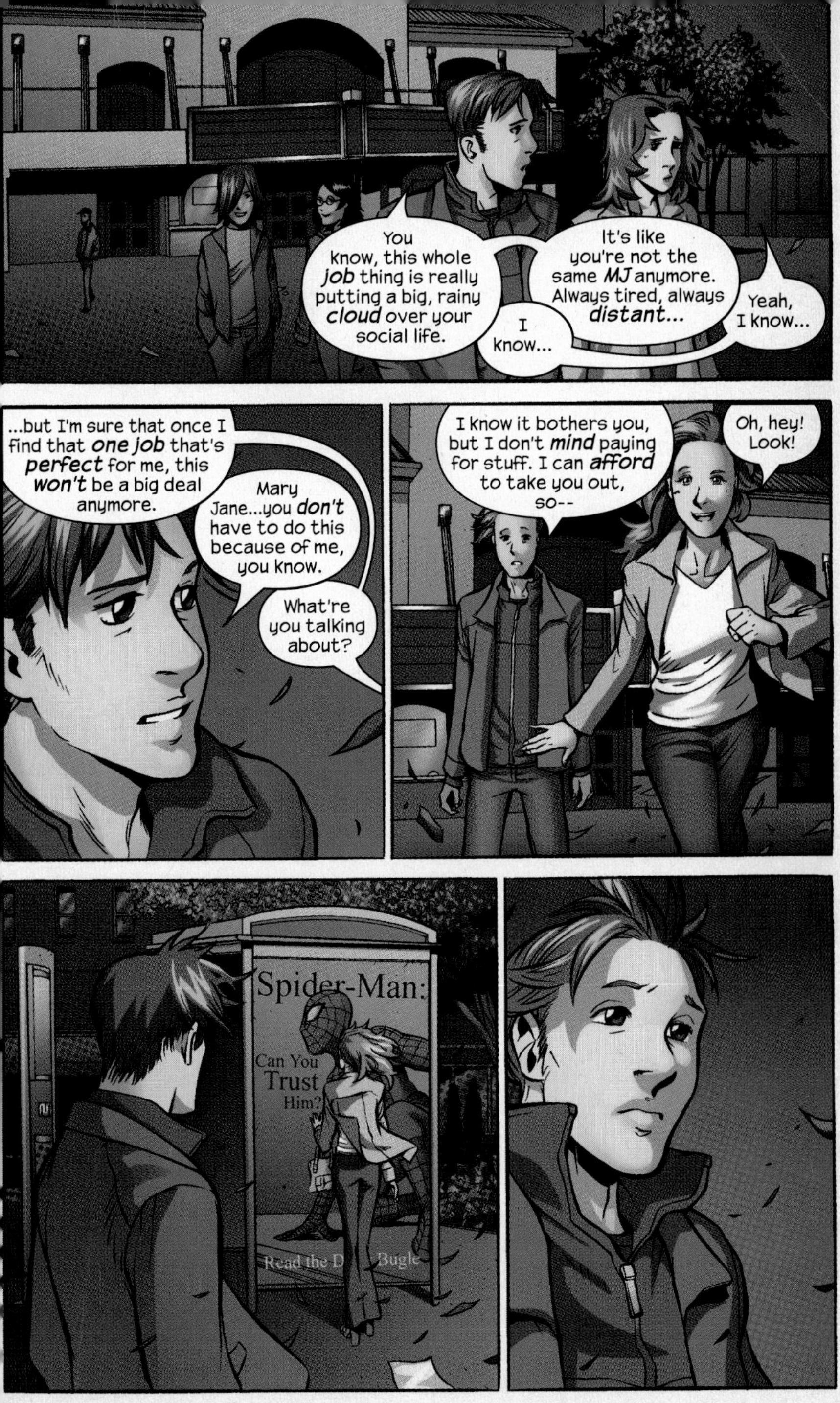

You know, this whole job thing is really putting a big, rainy cloud over your social life.
I know...
It's like you're not the same MJ anymore. Always tired, always distant...
Yeah, I know...
...but I'm sure that once I find that one job that's perfect for me, this won't be a big deal anymore.
Mary Jane...you don't have to do this because of me, you know.
What're you talking about?
I know it bothers you, but I don't mind paying for stuff. I can afford to take you out, so--
Oh, hey! Look!
Spider-Man:
Can You Trust Him?

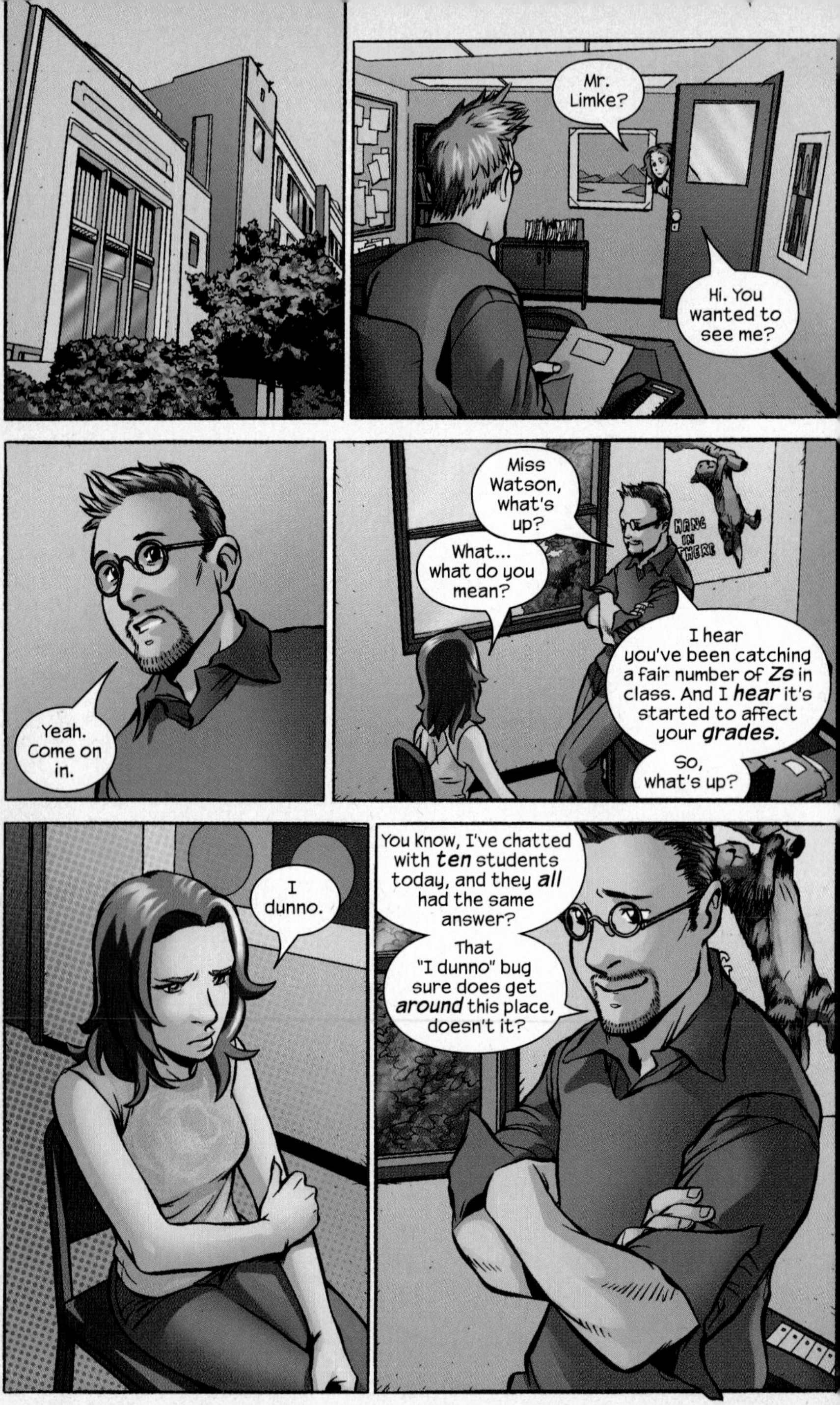
Mr. Limke?
Hi. You wanted to see me?
Yeah. Come on in.
Miss Watson, what's up?
What... what do you mean?
HANG IN THERE
I hear you've been catching a fair number of *Zs* in class. And I *hear* it's started to affect your *grades.*
So, what's up?
I dunno.
You know, I've chatted with *ten* students today, and they *all* had the same answer?
That "I dunno" bug sure does get *around* this place, doesn't it?

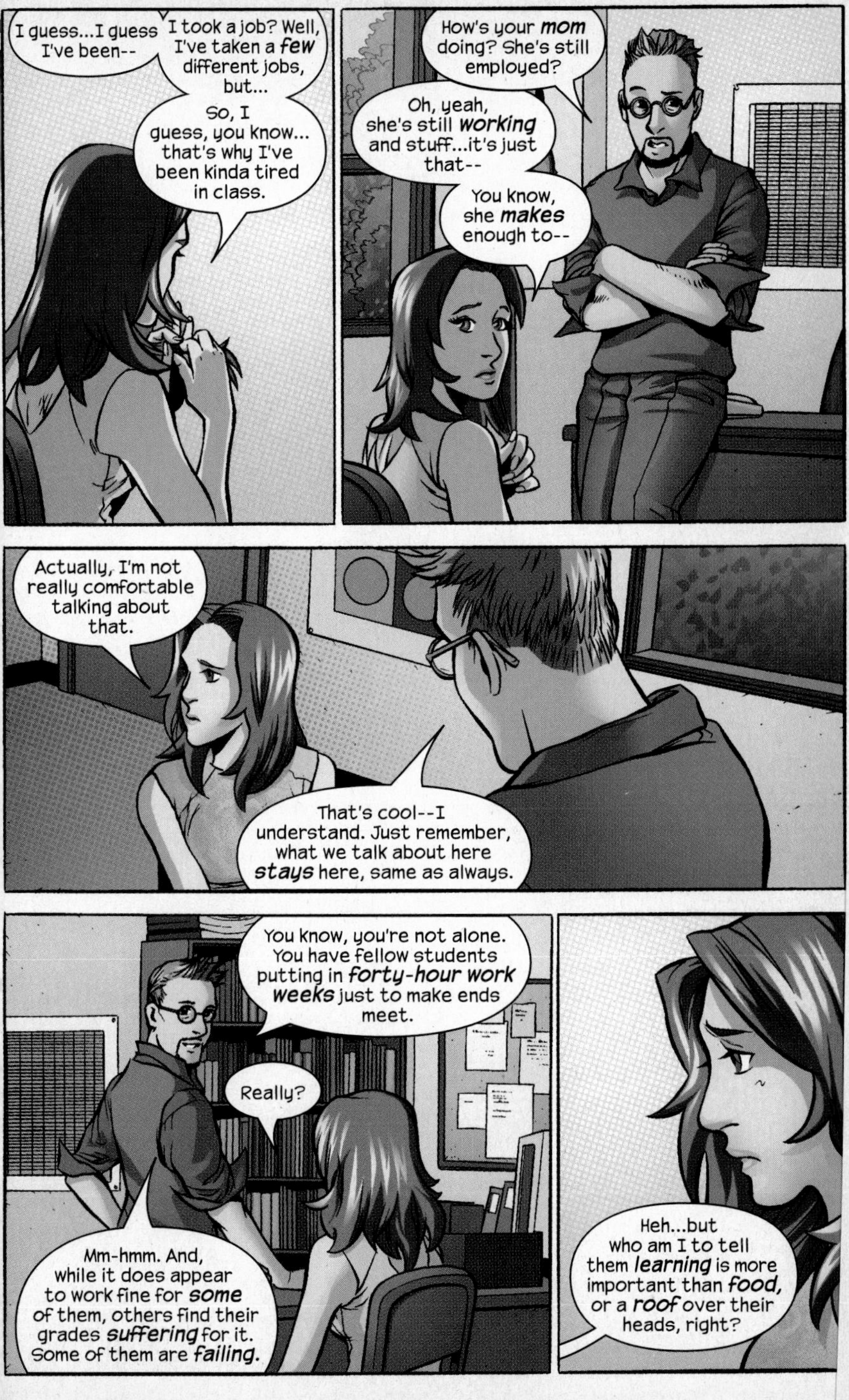
I guess...I guess I've been--
I took a job? Well, I've taken a few different jobs, but...
So, I guess, you know... that's why I've been kinda tired in class.
How's your mom doing? She's still employed?
Oh, yeah, she's still working and stuff...it's just that--
You know, she makes enough to--
Actually, I'm not really comfortable talking about that.
That's cool--I understand. Just remember, what we talk about here stays here, same as always.
You know, you're not alone. You have fellow students putting in forty-hour work weeks just to make ends meet.
Really?
Mm-hmm. And, while it does appear to work fine for some of them, others find their grades suffering for it. Some of them are failing.
Heh...but who am I to tell them learning is more important than food, or a roof over their heads, right?

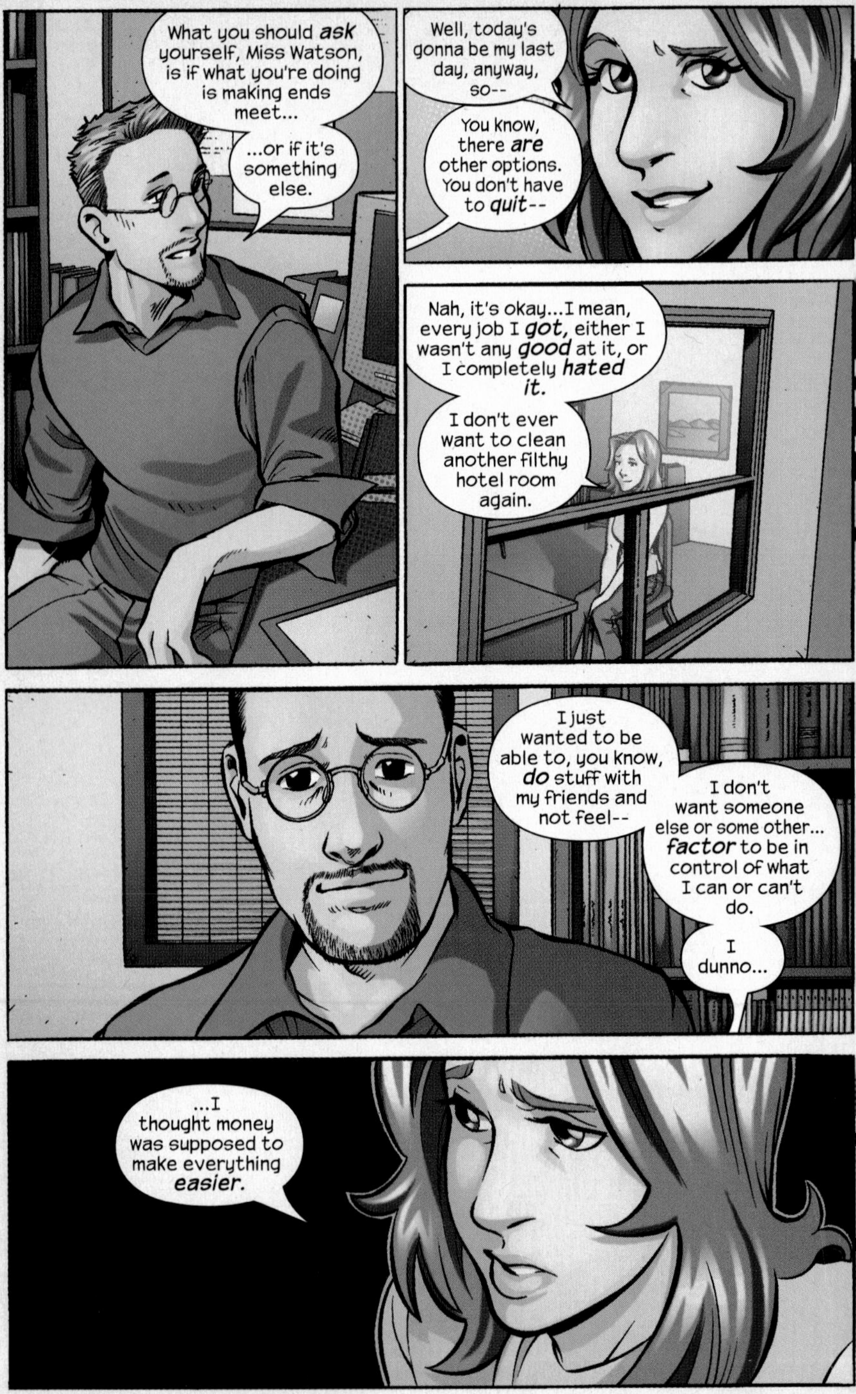

What you should *ask* yourself, Miss Watson, is if what you're doing is making ends meet...
...or if it's something else.
Well, today's gonna be my last day, anyway, so--
You know, there *are* other options. You don't have to *quit*--
Nah, it's okay...I mean, every job I *got,* either I wasn't any *good* at it, or I completely *hated* it.
I don't ever want to clean another filthy hotel room again.
I just wanted to be able to, you know, *do* stuff with my friends and not feel--
I don't want someone else or some other... *factor* to be in control of what I can or can't do.
I dunno...
...I thought money was supposed to make everything *easier.*

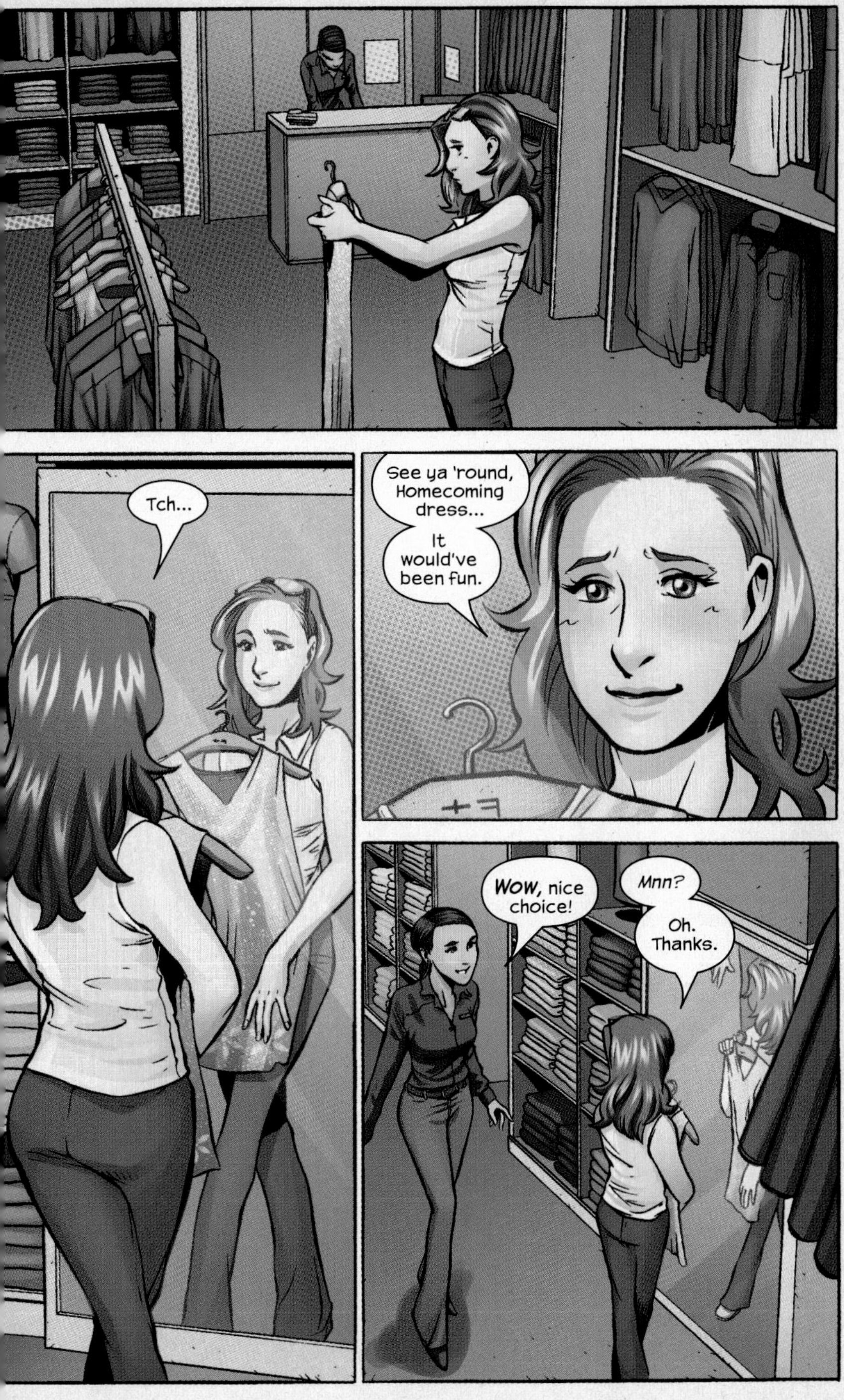
Tch...
See ya 'round, Homecoming dress...
It would've been fun.
WOW, nice choice!
Mnn?
Oh. Thanks.

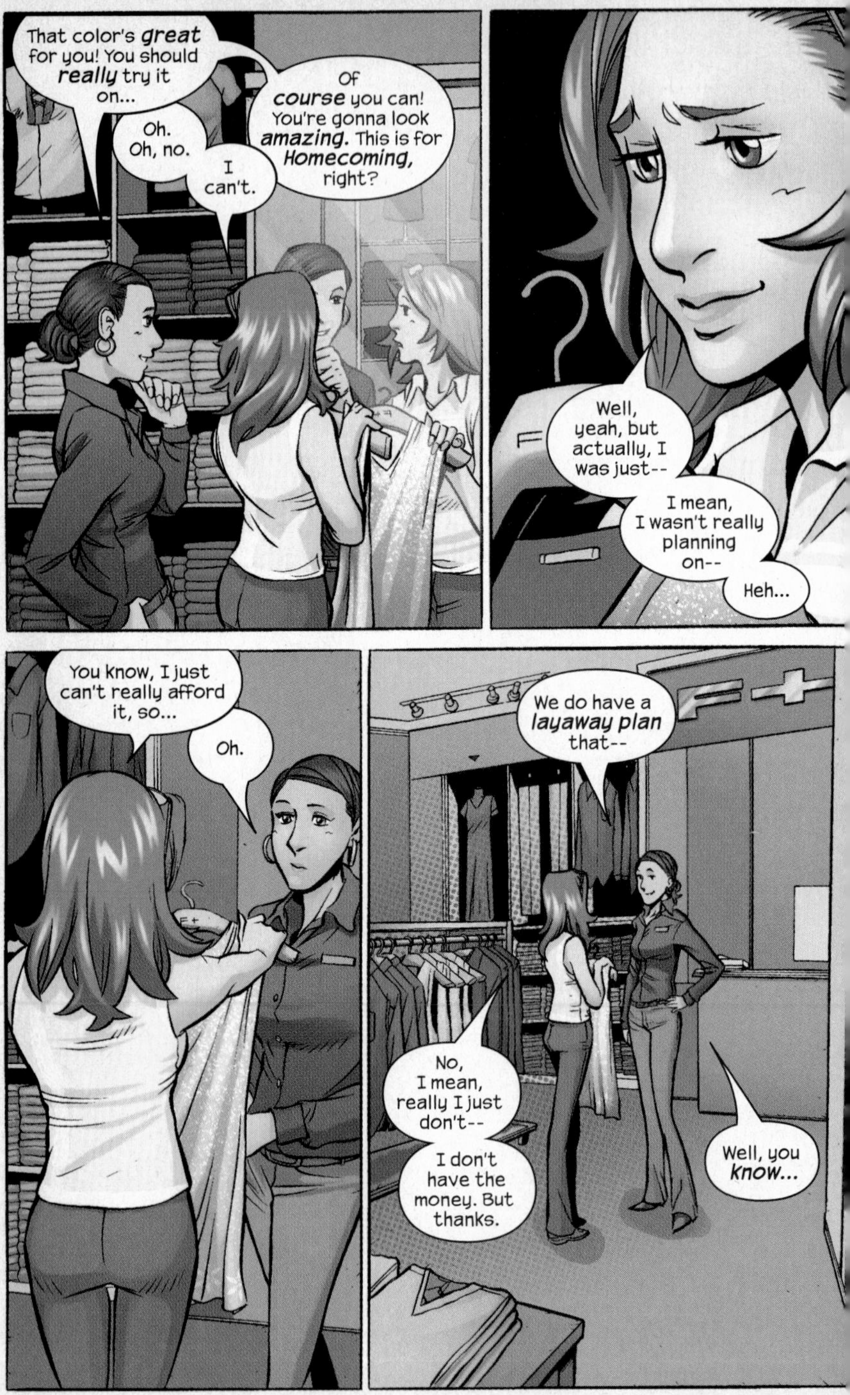
That color's *great* for you! You should *really* try it on...
Oh. Oh, no.
I can't.
Of *course* you can! You're gonna look *amazing.* This is for *Homecoming,* right?
Well, yeah, but actually, I was just--
I mean, I wasn't really planning on--
Heh...
You know, I just can't really afford it, so...
Oh.
We do have a *layaway plan* that--
No, I mean, really I just don't--
I don't have the money. But thanks.
Well, you *know...*

...you seem like a sweet girl, and one of my *salespeople* just went on *maternity leave.*

I was going to just *make do* without a replacement, but I *tell* ya, it's just *not* the same without a *second body* in here.

It's not a lot of *hours*, I'm afraid...

...but if you come in a few hours after school every couple days and help out, I'll *make sure* you have enough to buy that dress for Homecoming.

So? What do you think?

I think...

I think I'd like to put this on layaway, please.

THE MONEY THING

Sean Keever | Takeshi Miyazawa | Norman Lee | Christina Strain | Virtual Calligraphy's Randy Gentile | MacKenzie Cadenhead | C.B. Cebulski | Joe Quesada | Dan Buckley

Writer | Pencils | Inks | Colors | Letters | Editor | Consulting Editor | chief | Publisher

Special Thanks to David Gabriel

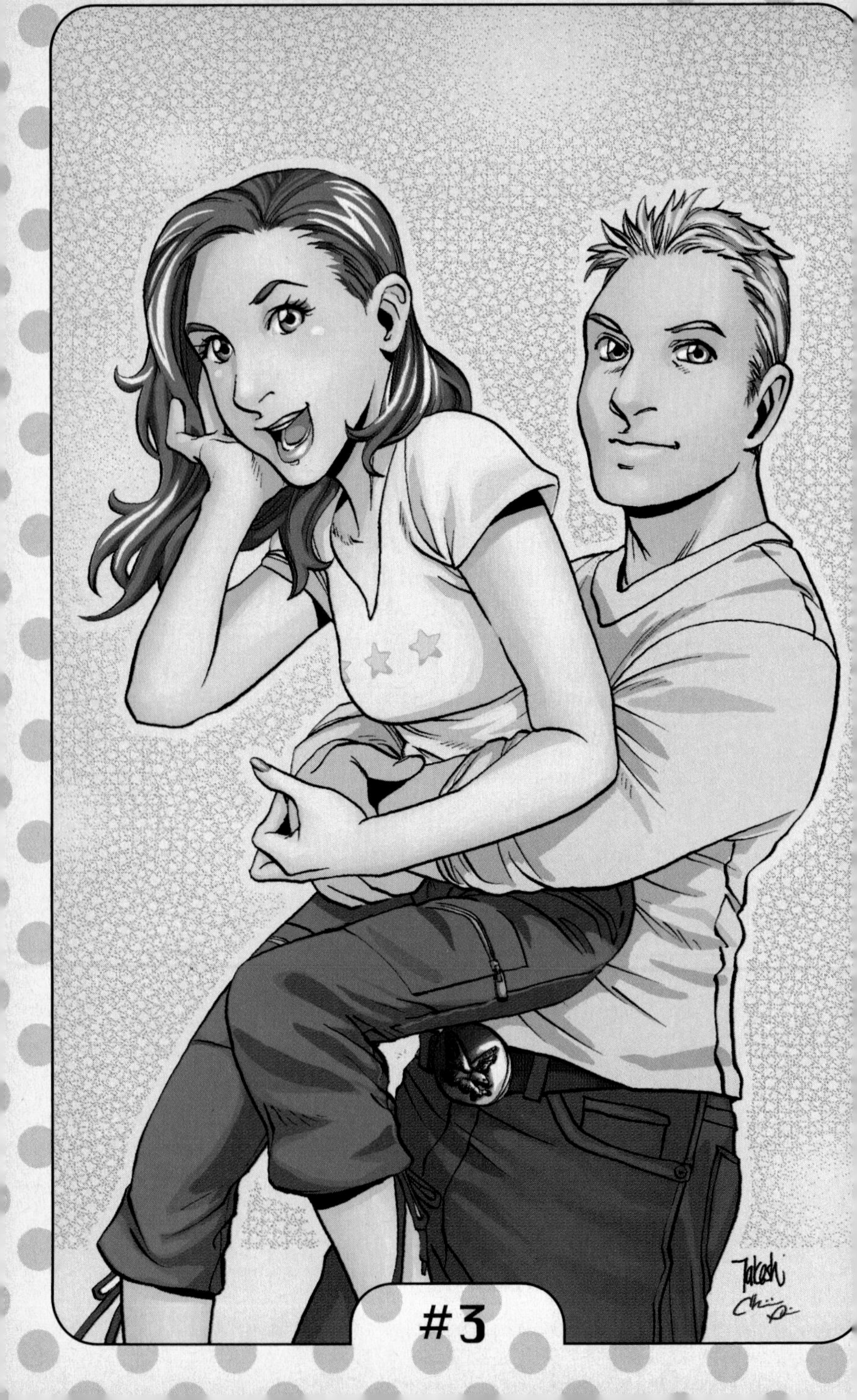

Takeshi
#3

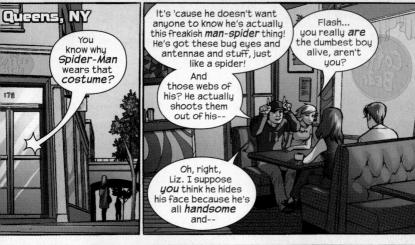

You know why **Spider-Man** wears that **costume**?

It's 'cause he doesn't want anyone to know he's actually this freakish **man-spider** thing! He's got these bug eyes and antennae and stuff, just like a spider!

And those webs of his? He actually shoots them out of his--

Flash... you really **are** the dumbest boy alive, aren't you?

Oh, right, Liz. I suppose **you** think he hides his face because he's all **handsome** and--

Could we **please** not talk about Spider-Man?

Oh my gosh...

What?

Those two.

They're the most hyper, annoying **bozos** in the entire school. It's like all they do is play **pranks** on me all day. Geez...the **last** thing they need is more caffeine and sugar.

I hope they don't see me...

Really? I don't think I've ever even **seen** them before...

What do they **do** to ya, MJ?

Well, let's see...

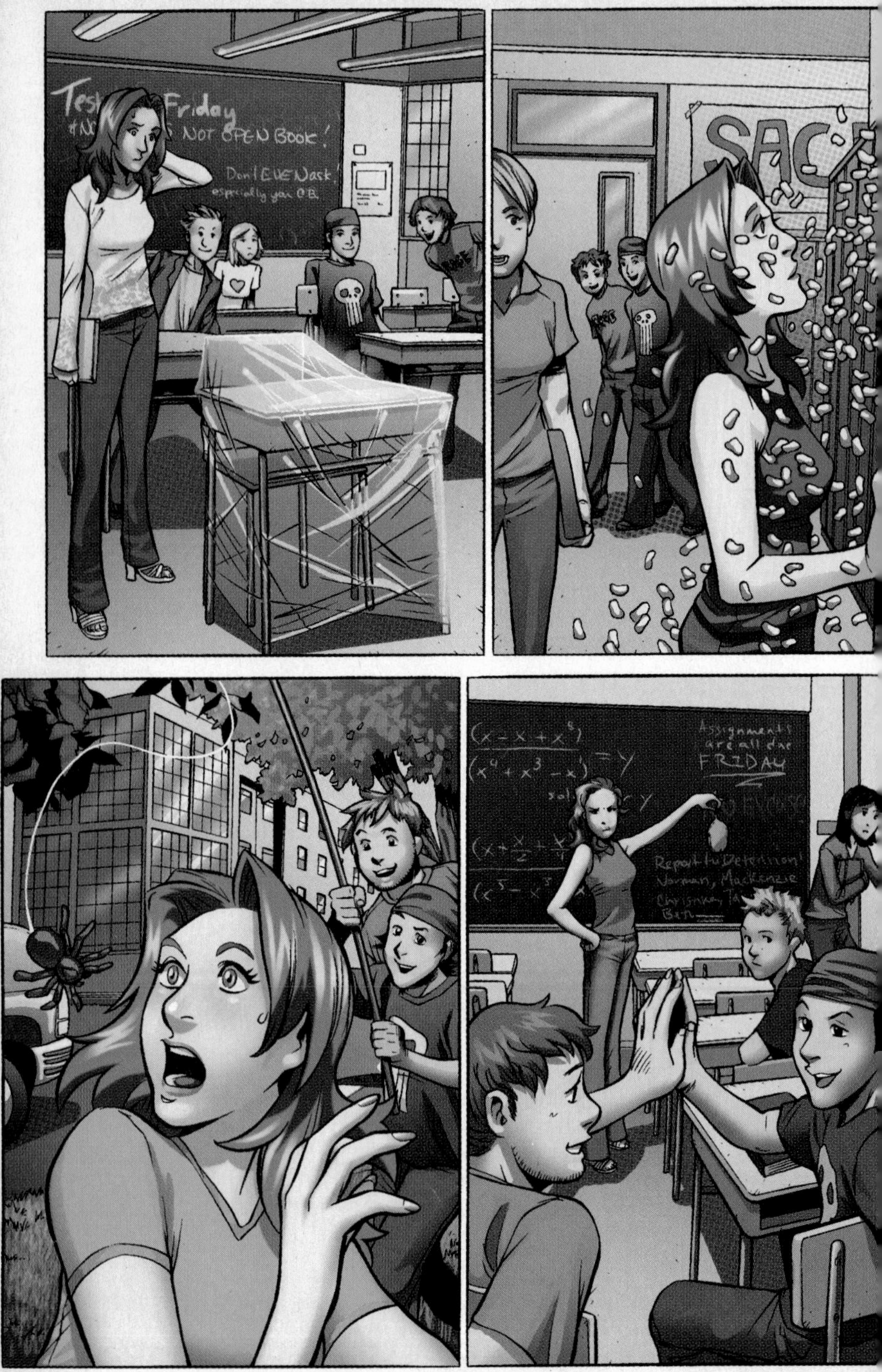
Friday
NOT OPEN Book!
Don't EVEN ask!
especially you C.B.
SAC
Assignments are all due FRIDAY
Report to Detention!

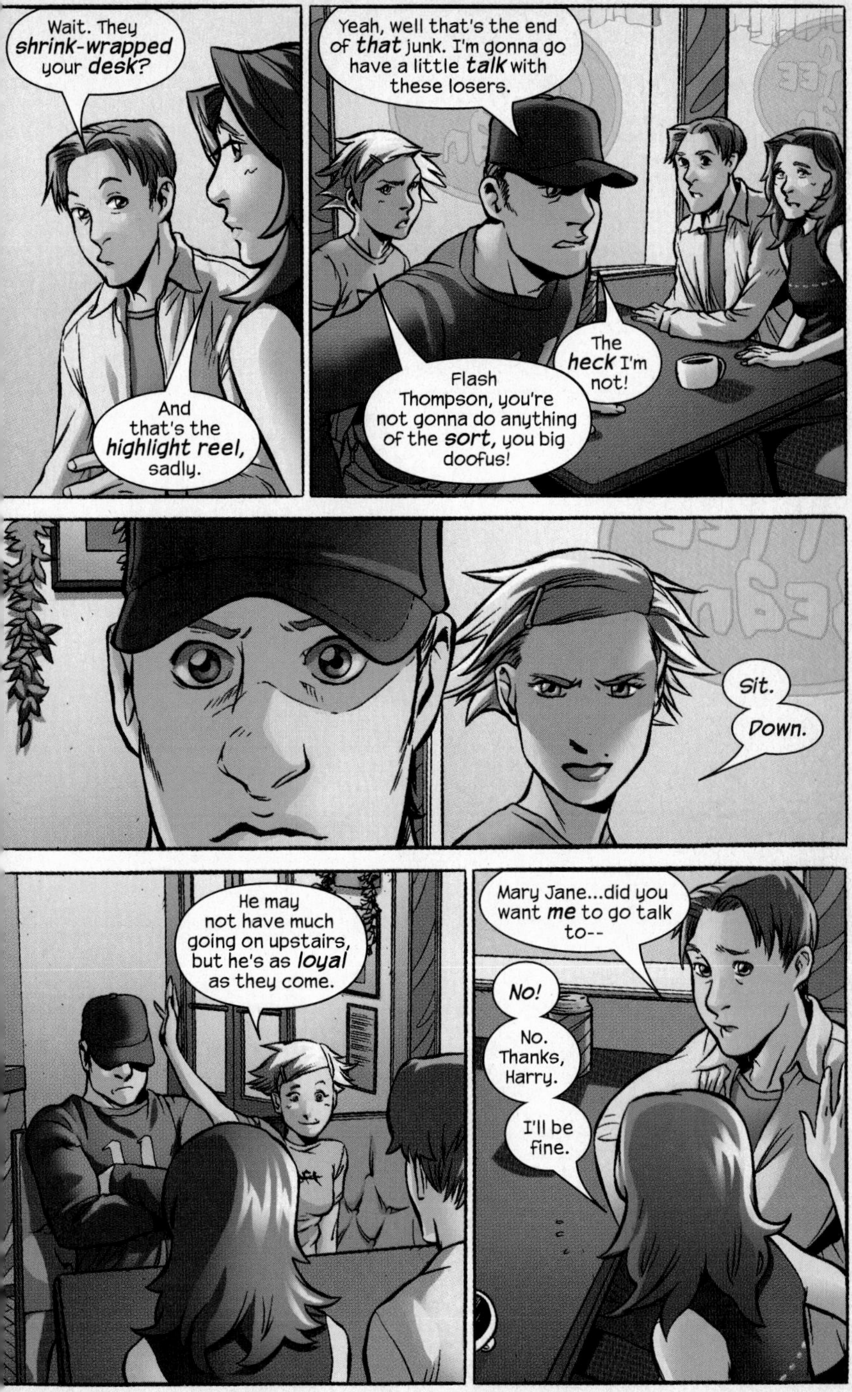
Wait. They shrink-wrapped your desk?
And that's the highlight reel, sadly.
Yeah, well that's the end of that junk. I'm gonna go have a little talk with these losers.
Flash Thompson, you're not gonna do anything of the sort, you big doofus!
The heck I'm not!
Sit.
Down.
He may not have much going on upstairs, but he's as loyal as they come.
Mary Jane...did you want me to go talk to--
No!
No. Thanks, Harry.
I'll be fine.

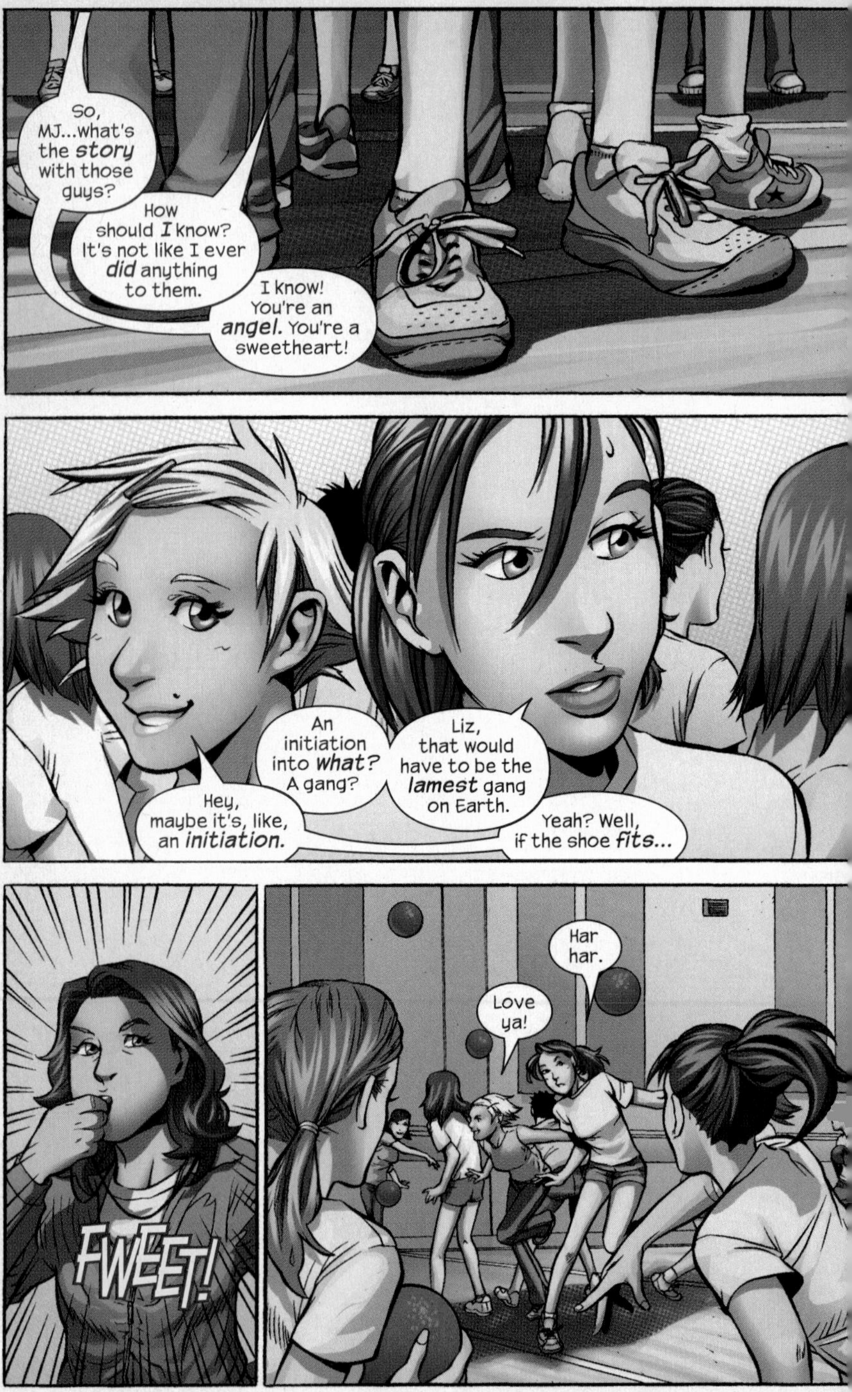
So, MJ...what's the *story* with those guys?
How should *I* know? It's not like I ever *did* anything to them.
I know! You're an *angel.* You're a sweetheart!
Hey, maybe it's, like, an *initiation.*
An initiation into *what?* A gang?
Liz, that would have to be the *lamest* gang on Earth.
Yeah? Well, if the shoe *fits...*
FWEET!
Har har.
Love ya!

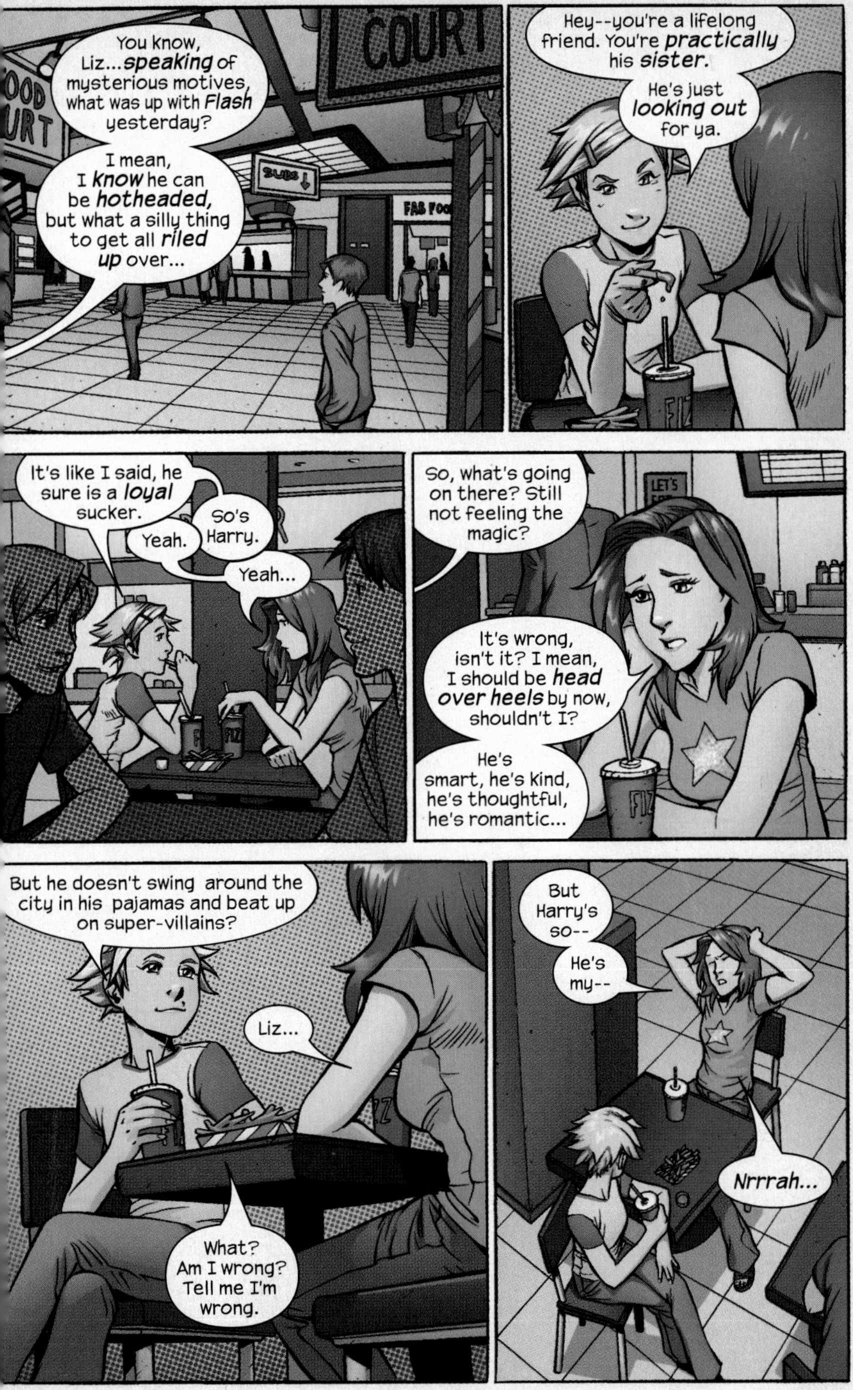

COURT
You know, Liz...speaking of mysterious motives, what was up with Flash yesterday?
I mean, I know he can be hotheaded, but what a silly thing to get all riled up over...
Hey--you're a lifelong friend. You're practically his sister.
He's just looking out for ya.
It's like I said, he sure is a loyal sucker.
Yeah.
So's Harry.
Yeah...
So, what's going on there? Still not feeling the magic?
It's wrong, isn't it? I mean, I should be head over heels by now, shouldn't I?
He's smart, he's kind, he's thoughtful, he's romantic...
But he doesn't swing around the city in his pajamas and beat up on super-villains?
Liz...
What? Am I wrong? Tell me I'm wrong.
But Harry's so--
He's my--
Nrrrah...

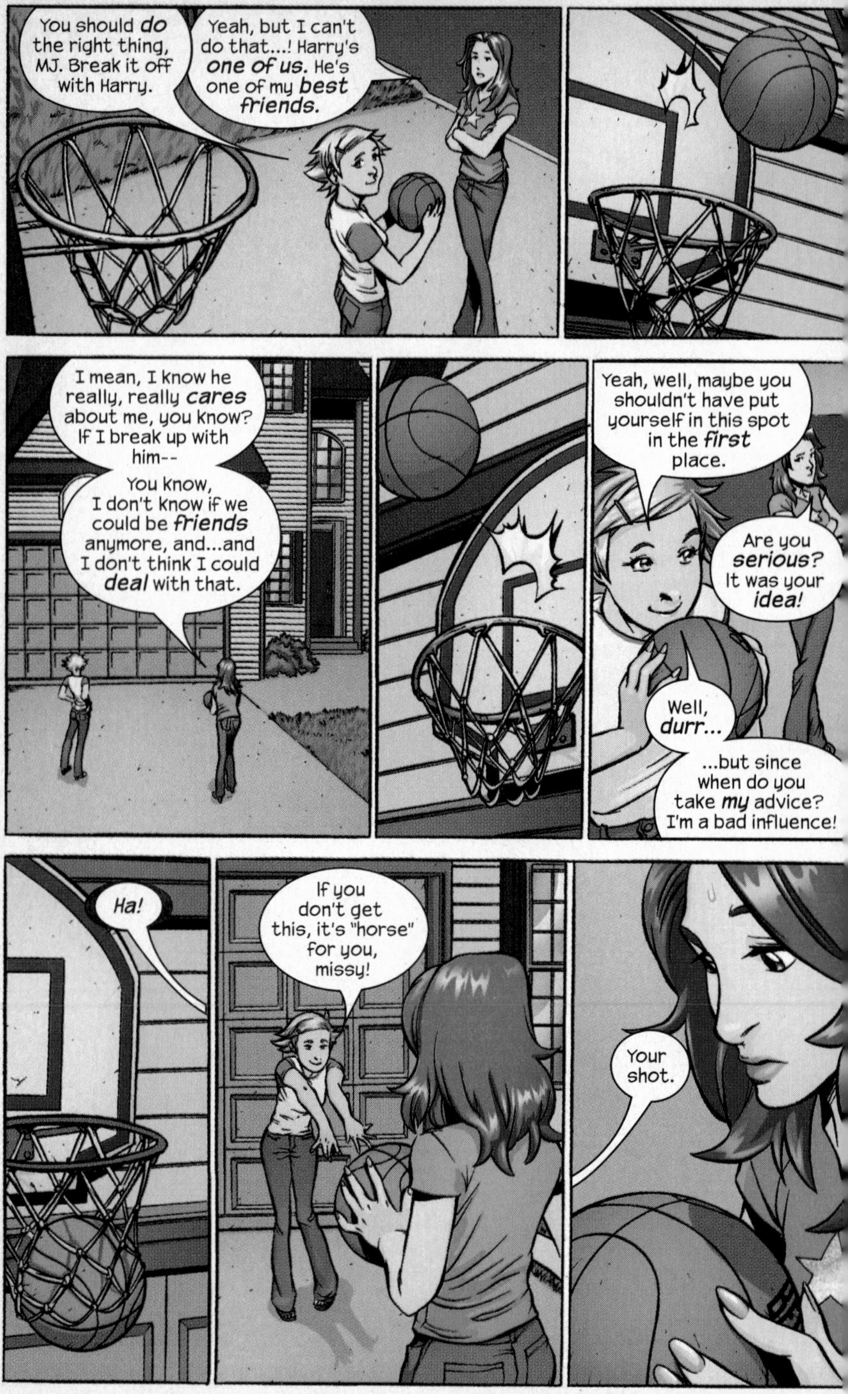
You should *do* the right thing, MJ. Break it off with Harry.
Yeah, but I can't do that...! Harry's *one of us.* He's one of my *best friends.*
I mean, I know he really, really *cares* about me, you know? If I break up with him--
You know, I don't know if we could be *friends* anymore, and...and I don't think I could *deal* with that.
Yeah, well, maybe you shouldn't have put yourself in this spot in the *first* place.
Are you *serious?* It was your *idea!*
Well, *durr...*
...but since when do you take *my* advice? I'm a bad influence!
Ha!
If you don't get this, it's "horse" for you, missy!
Your shot.

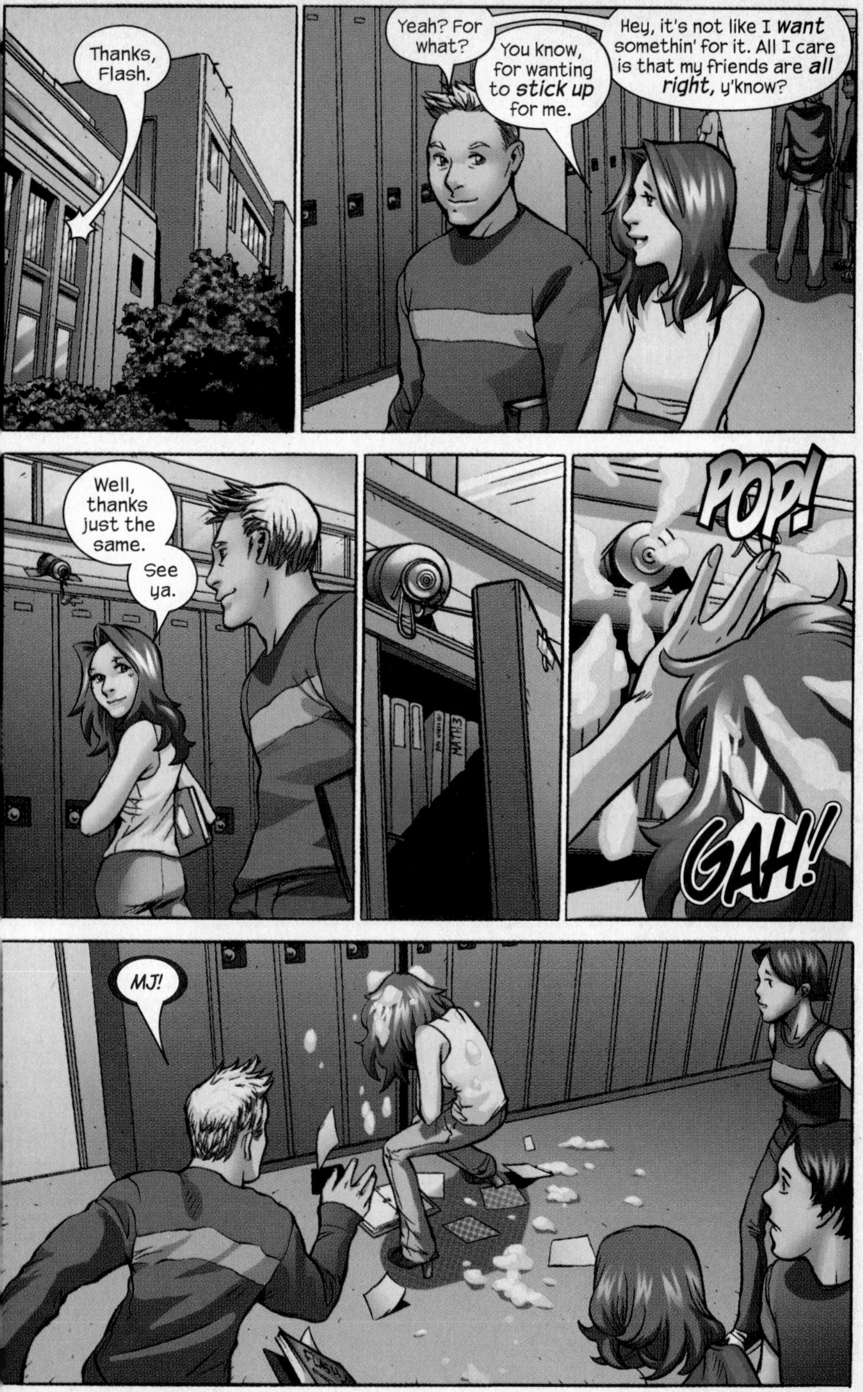
Thanks, Flash.
Yeah? For what?
You know, for wanting to stick up for me.
Hey, it's not like I want somethin' for it. All I care is that my friends are all right, y'know?
Well, thanks just the same.
See ya.
MATH3
POP!
GAH!
MJ!

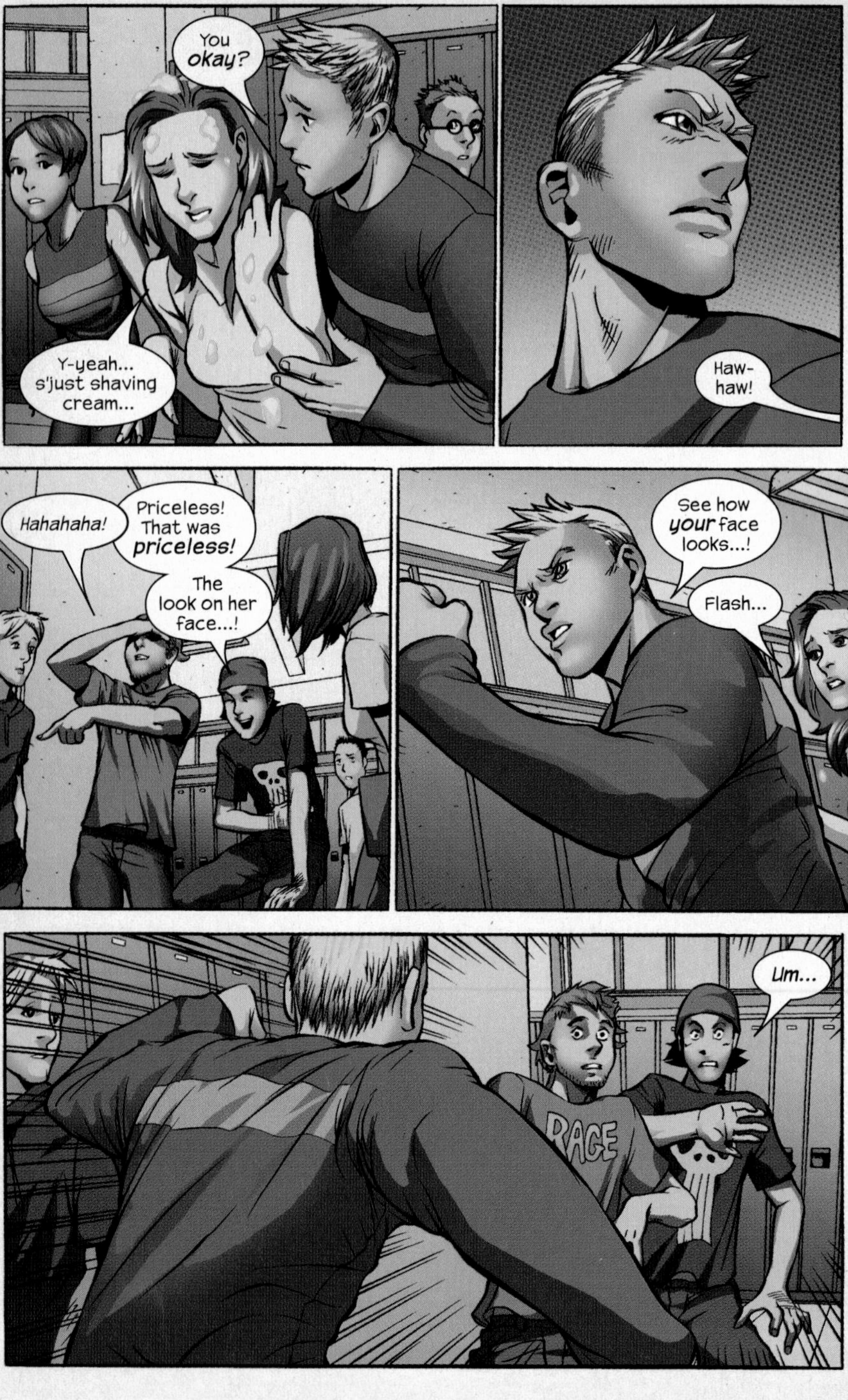
You okay?
Y-yeah... s'just shaving cream...
Haw-haw!
Hahahaha!
Priceless! That was priceless!
The look on her face...!
See how your face looks...!
Flash...
Um...

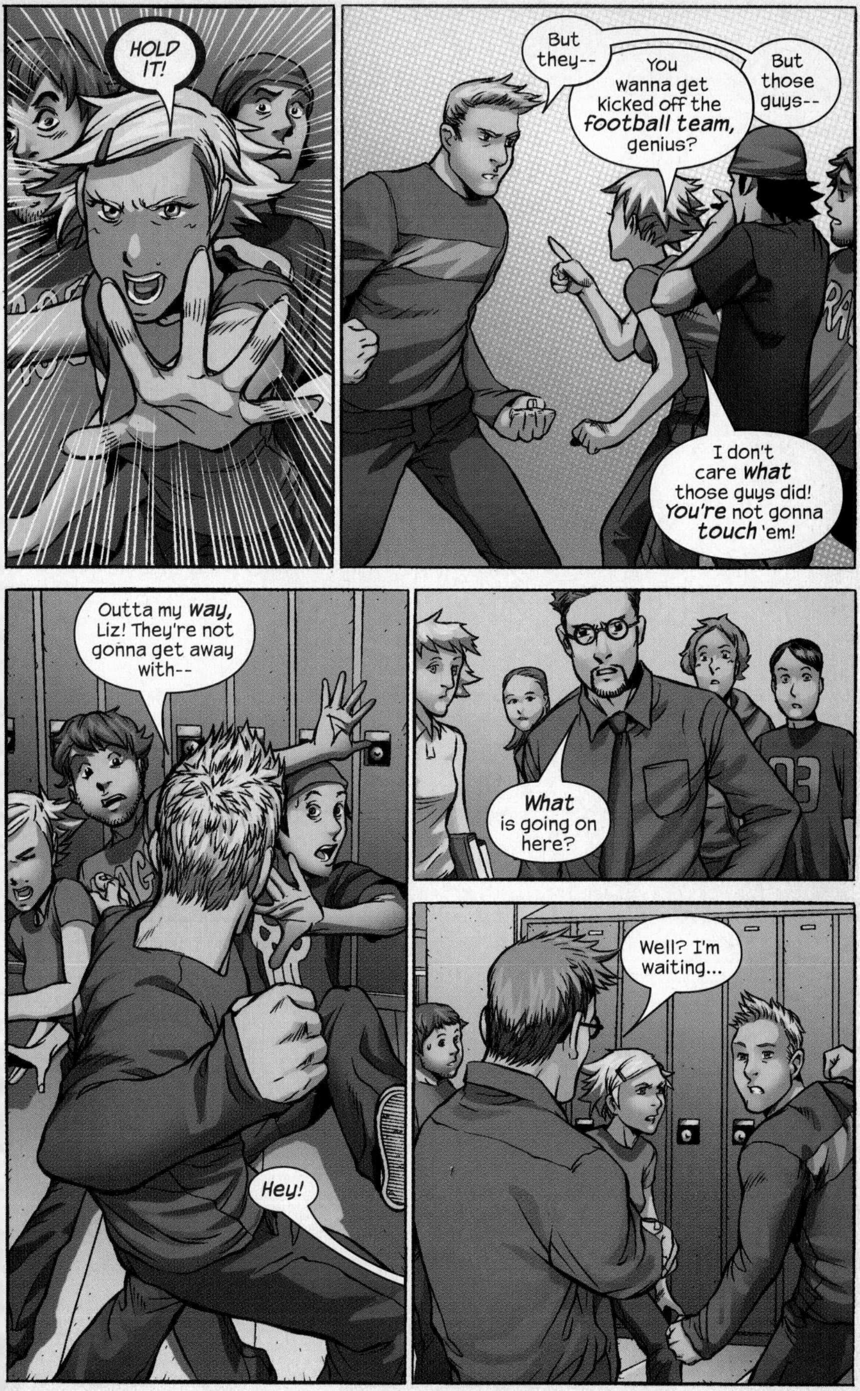
HOLD IT!
But they--
You wanna get kicked off the football team, genius?
But those guys--
I don't care what those guys did! You're not gonna touch 'em!
Outta my way, Liz! They're not gonna get away with--
Hey!
What is going on here?
Well? I'm waiting...

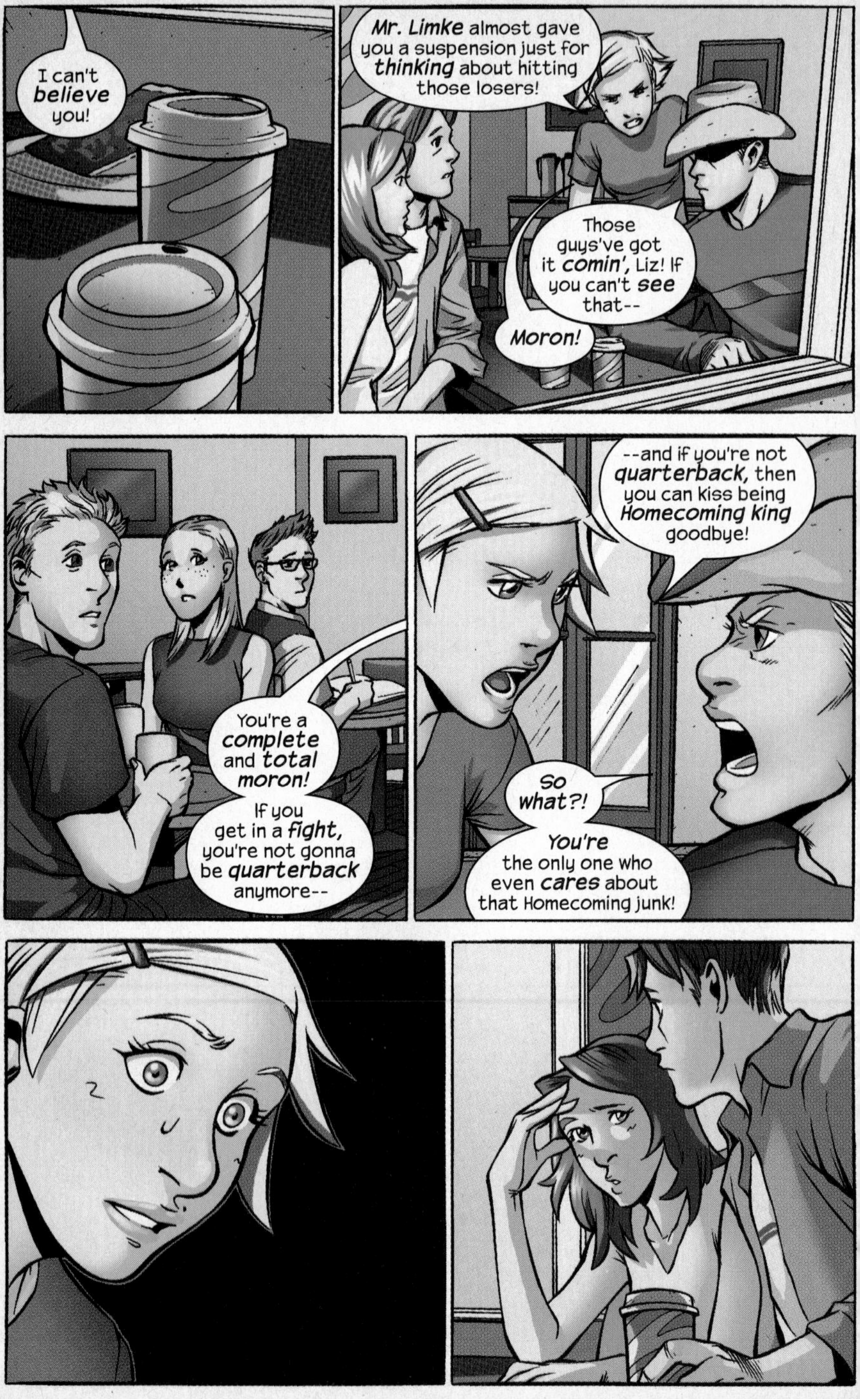
I can't believe you!
Mr. Limke almost gave you a suspension just for thinking about hitting those losers!
Those guys've got it comin', Liz! If you can't see that--
Moron!
You're a complete and total moron!
If you get in a fight, you're not gonna be quarterback anymore--
--and if you're not quarterback, then you can kiss being Homecoming king goodbye!
So what?!
You're the only one who even cares about that Homecoming junk!

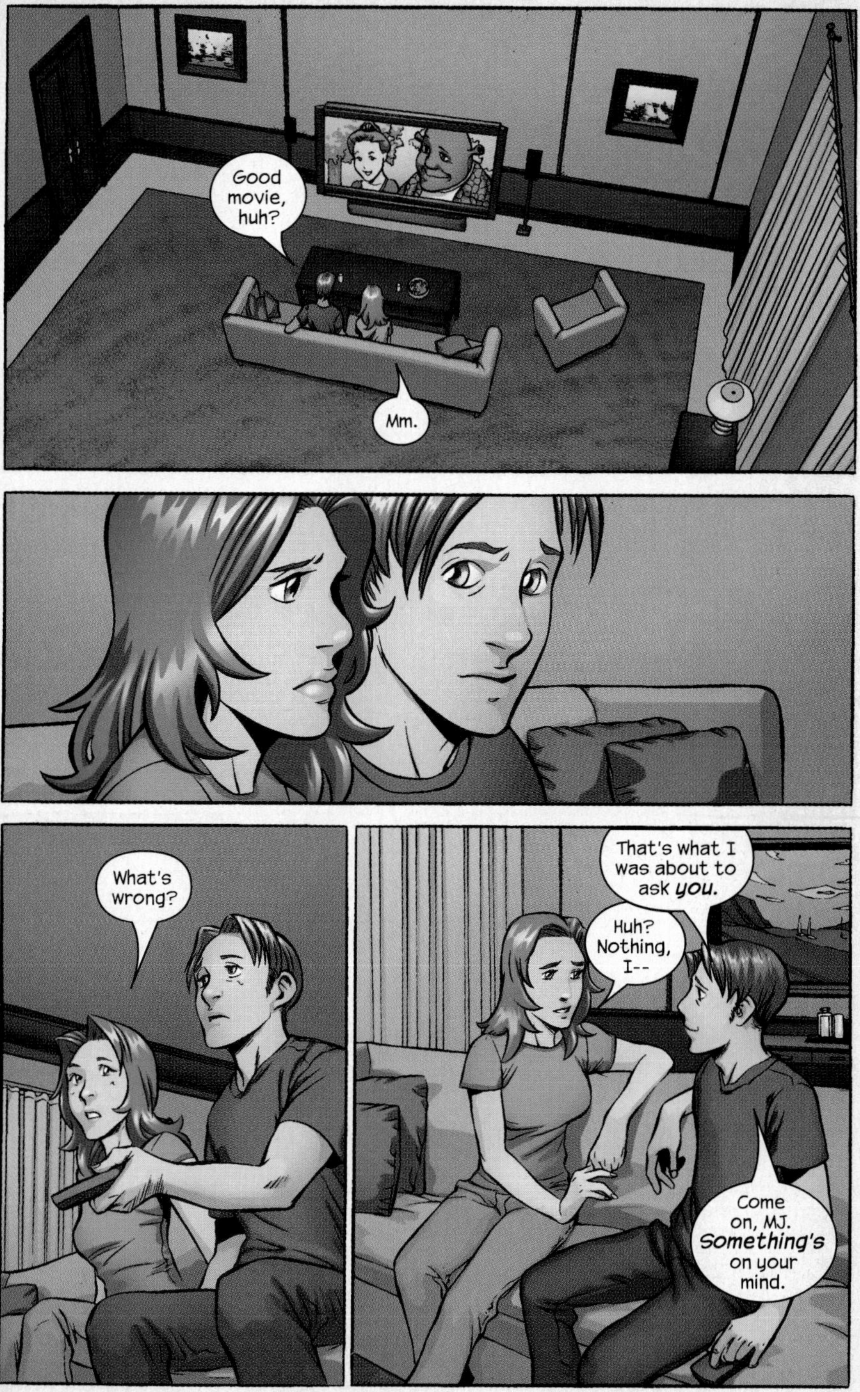
Good movie, huh?
Mm.
What's wrong?
That's what I was about to ask you.
Huh? Nothing, I--
Come on, MJ. Something's on your mind.

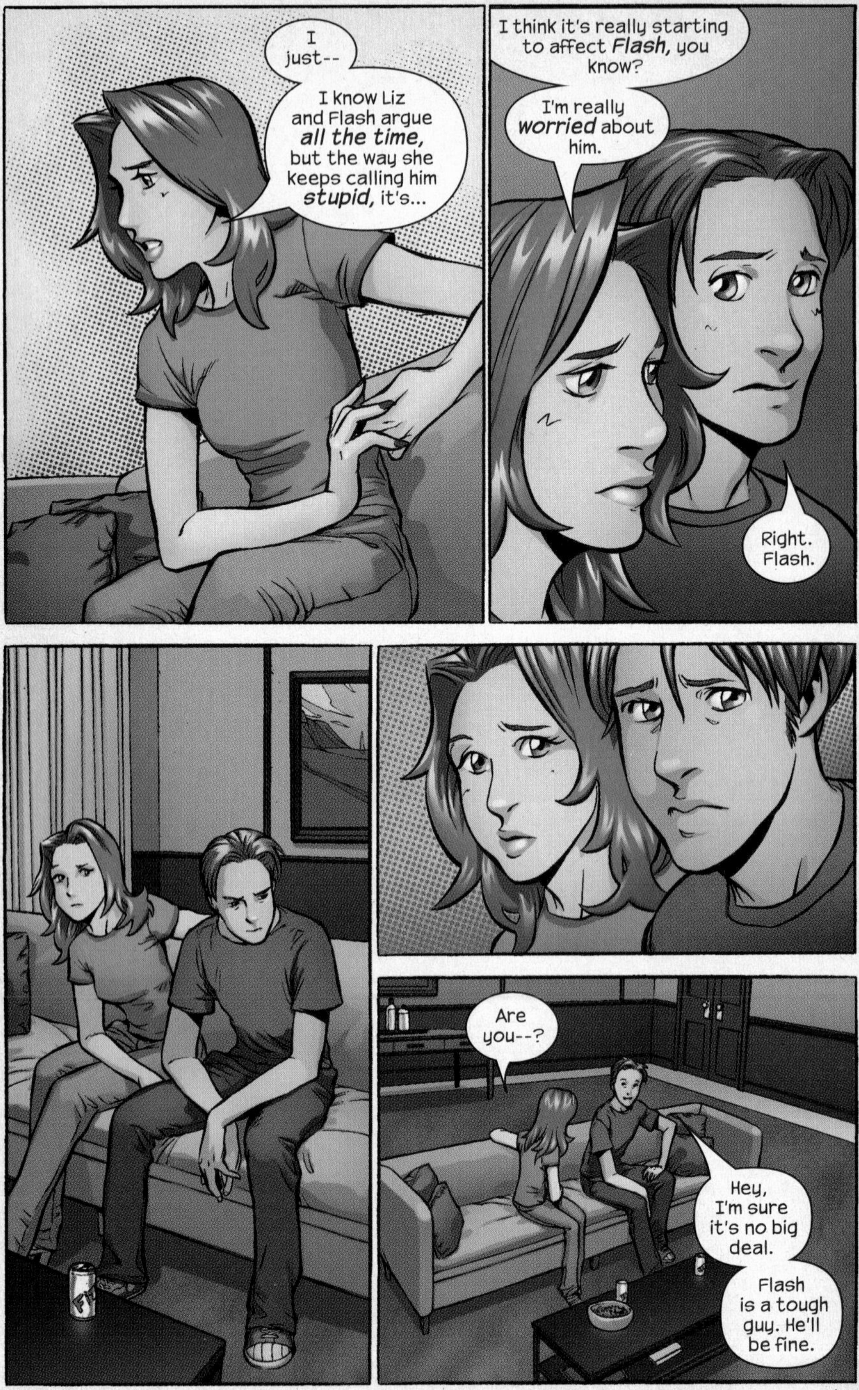
I just--
I know Liz and Flash argue all the time, but the way she keeps calling him stupid, it's...
I think it's really starting to affect Flash, you know?
I'm really worried about him.
Right. Flash.
Are you--?
Hey, I'm sure it's no big deal.
Flash is a tough guy. He'll be fine.

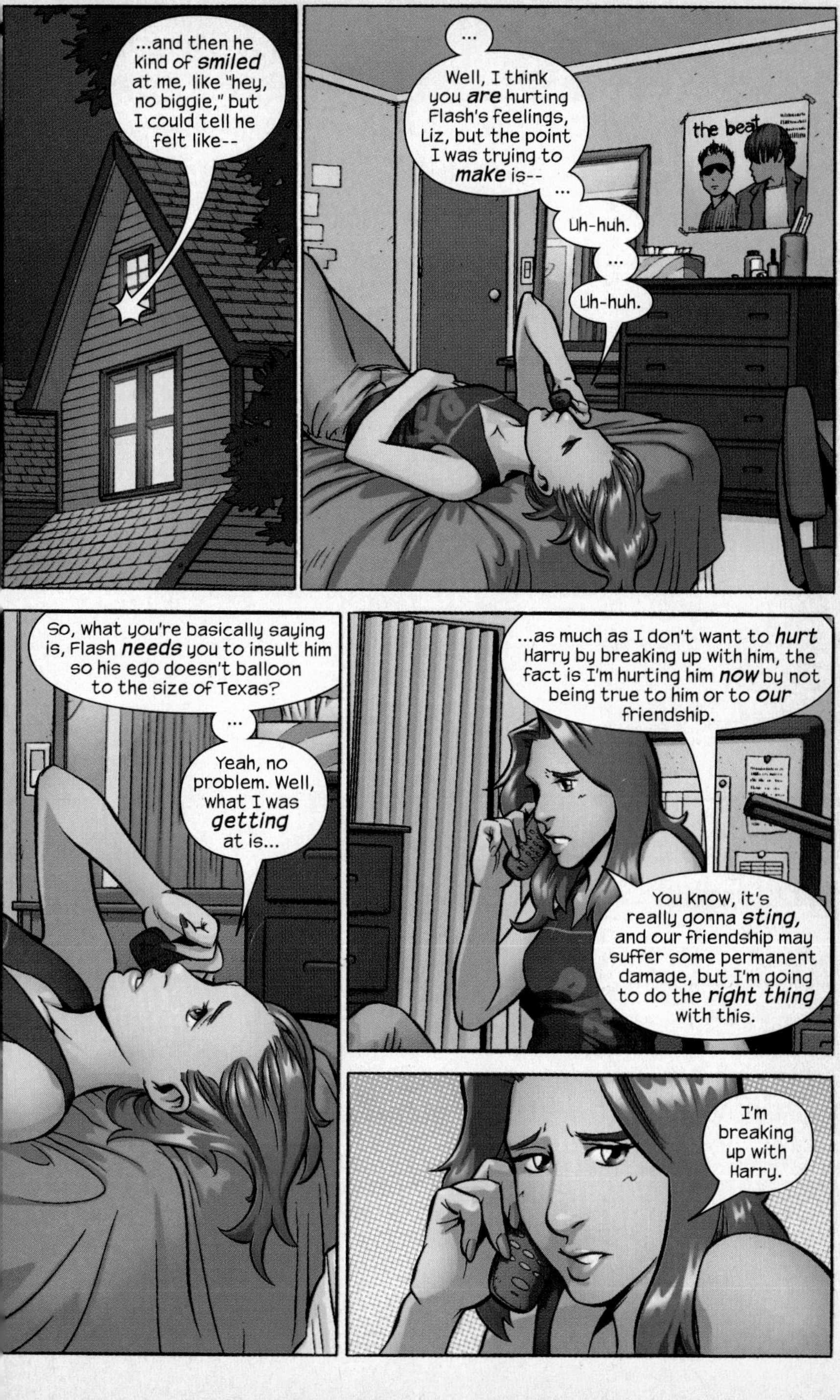
...and then he kind of smiled at me, like "hey, no biggie," but I could tell he felt like--
...
Well, I think you are hurting Flash's feelings, Liz, but the point I was trying to make is--
...
Uh-huh.
...
Uh-huh.
the beat
So, what you're basically saying is, Flash needs you to insult him so his ego doesn't balloon to the size of Texas?
...
Yeah, no problem. Well, what I was getting at is...
...as much as I don't want to hurt Harry by breaking up with him, the fact is I'm hurting him now by not being true to him or to our friendship.
You know, it's really gonna sting, and our friendship may suffer some permanent damage, but I'm going to do the right thing with this.
I'm breaking up with Harry.

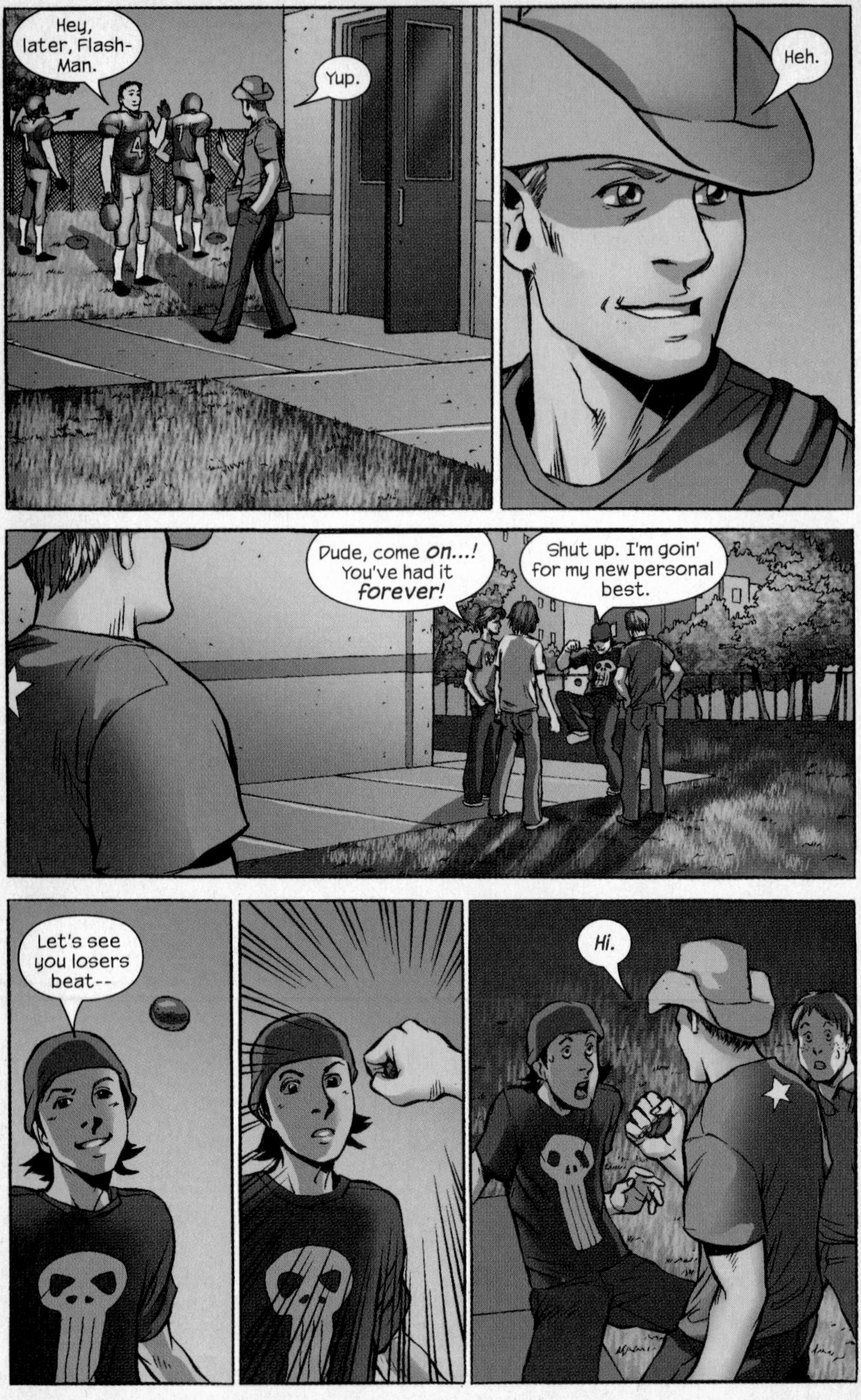
Hey, later, Flash-Man.
Yup.
Heh.
Dude, come on...! You've had it forever!
Shut up. I'm goin' for my new personal best.
Let's see you losers beat--
Hi.

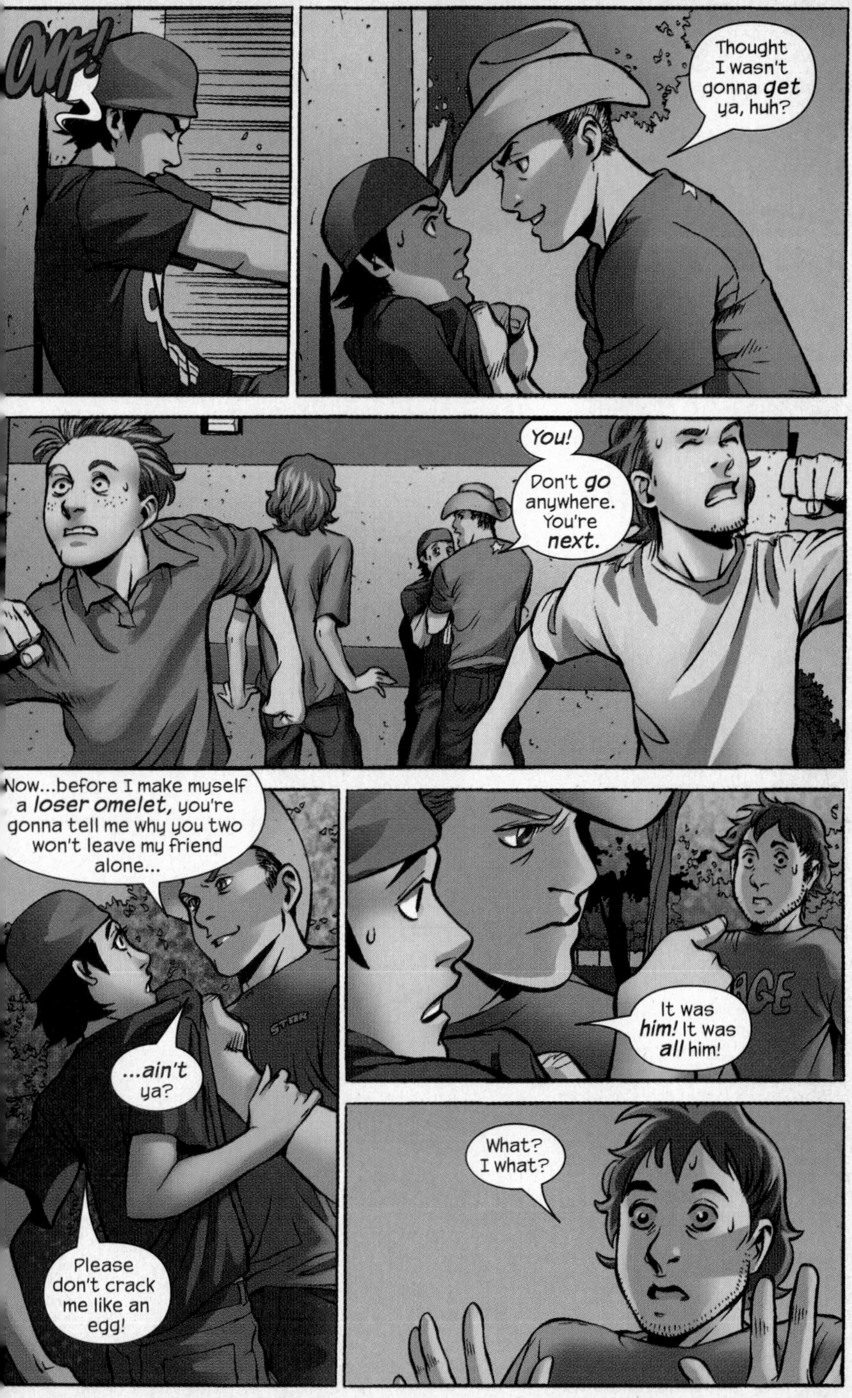
OWF!
Thought I wasn't gonna get ya, huh?
You!
Don't go anywhere. You're next.
Now...before I make myself a loser omelet, you're gonna tell me why you two won't leave my friend alone...
...ain't ya?
Please don't crack me like an egg!
It was him! It was all him!
What? I what?

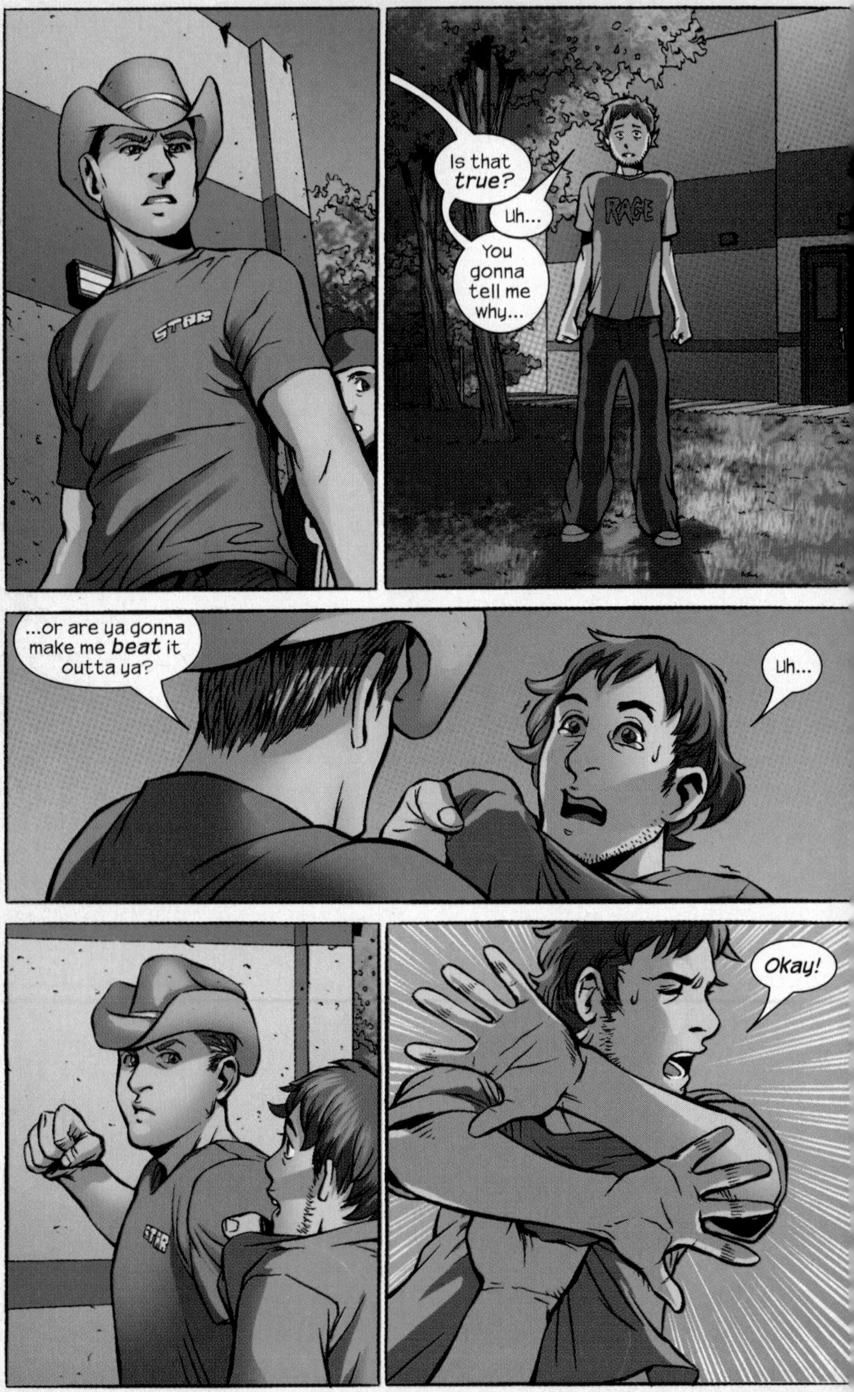
Is that true?
Uh...
You gonna tell me why...
...or are ya gonna make me beat it outta ya?
Uh...
Okay!

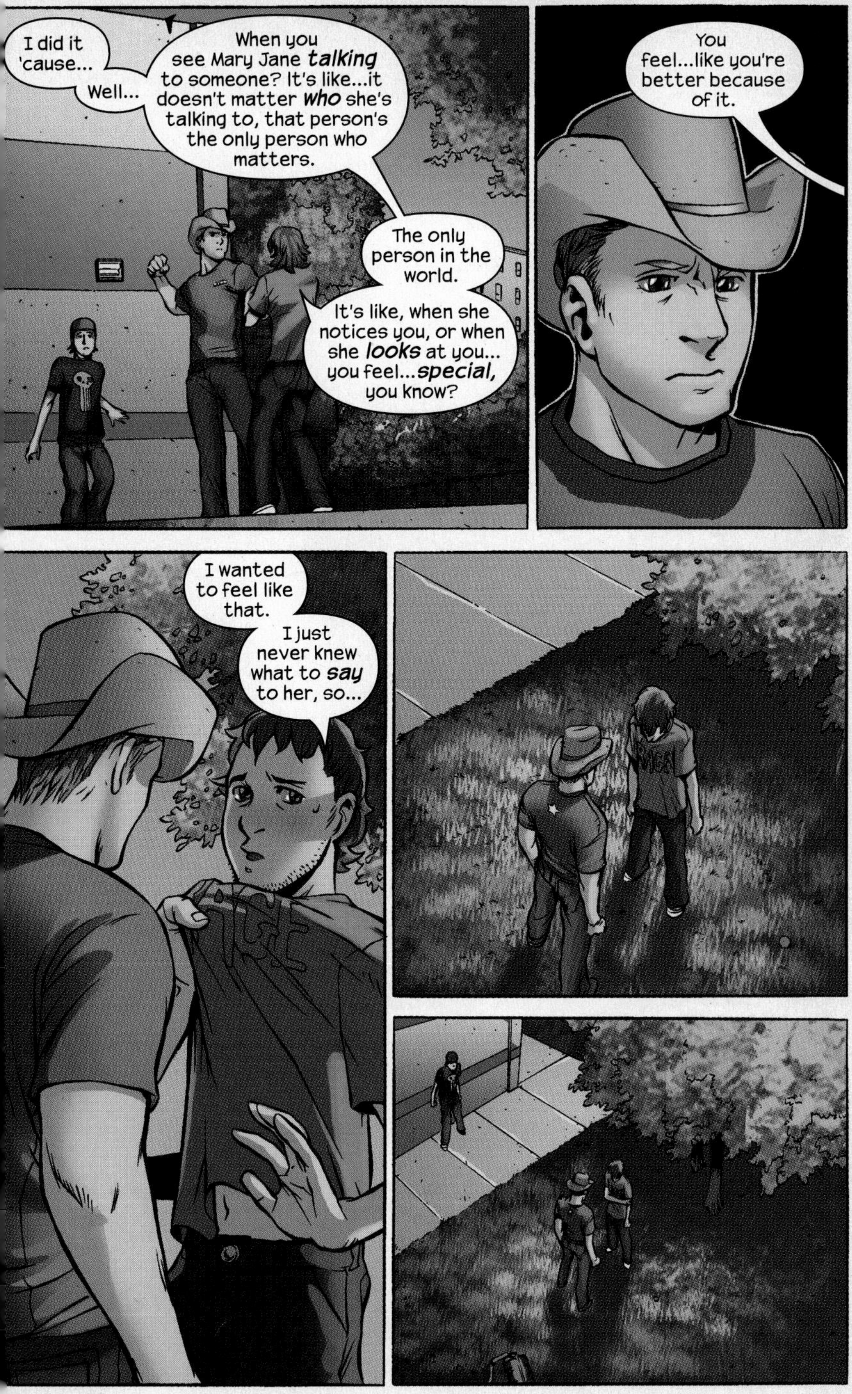
I did it 'cause...
Well...
When you see Mary Jane *talking* to someone? It's like...it doesn't matter *who* she's talking to, that person's the only person who matters.
The only person in the world.
It's like, when she notices you, or when she *looks* at you... you feel...*special,* you know?
You feel...like you're better because of it.
I wanted to feel like that.
I just never knew what to *say* to her, so...

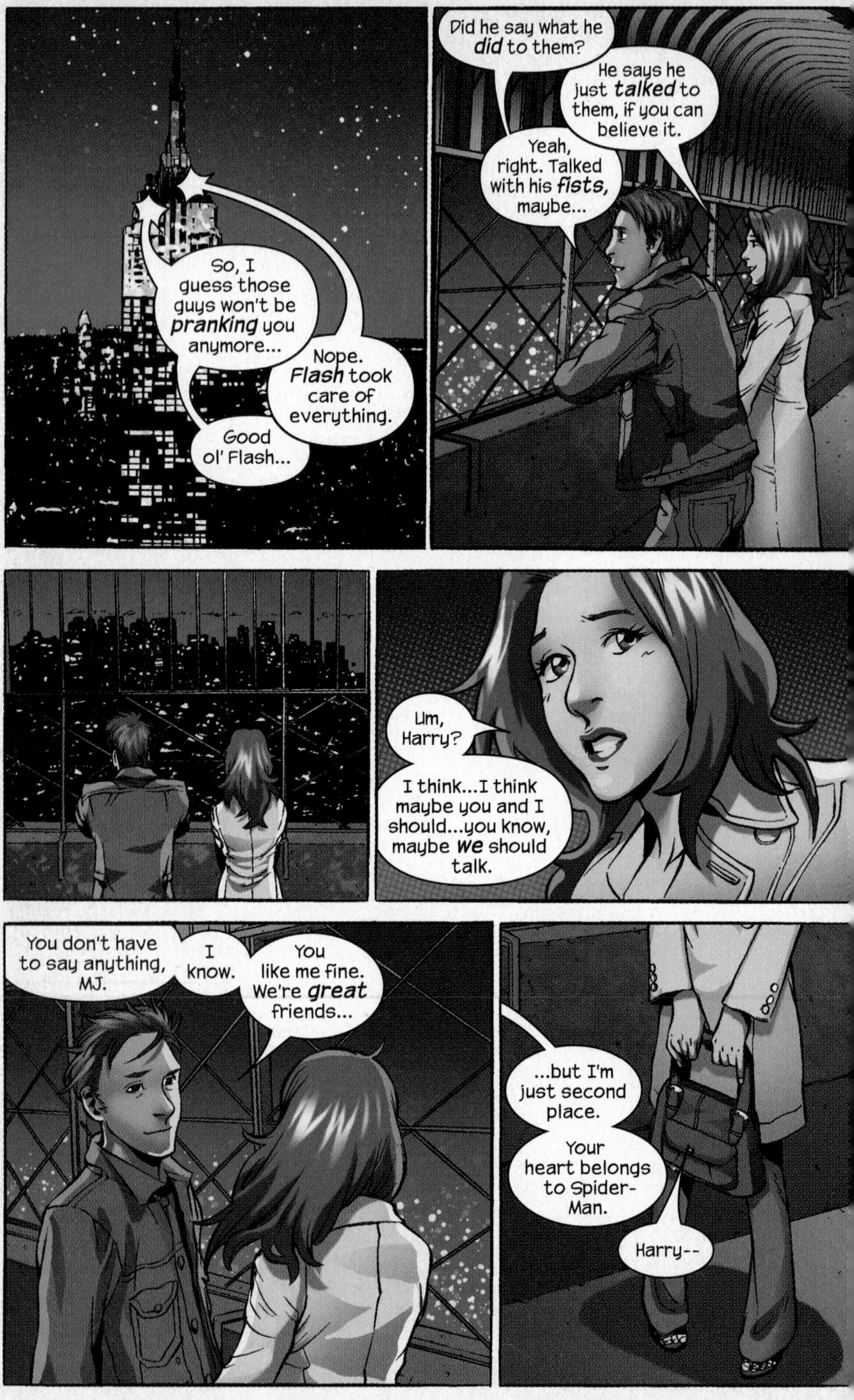

So, I guess those guys won't be *pranking* you anymore...
Nope. *Flash* took care of everything.
Good ol' Flash...
Did he say what he *did* to them?
He says he just *talked* to them, if you can believe it.
Yeah, right. Talked with his *fists,* maybe...
Um, Harry?
I think...I think maybe you and I should...you know, maybe *we* should talk.
You don't have to say anything, MJ.
I know.
You like me fine. We're *great* friends...
...but I'm just second place.
Your heart belongs to Spider-Man.
Harry--

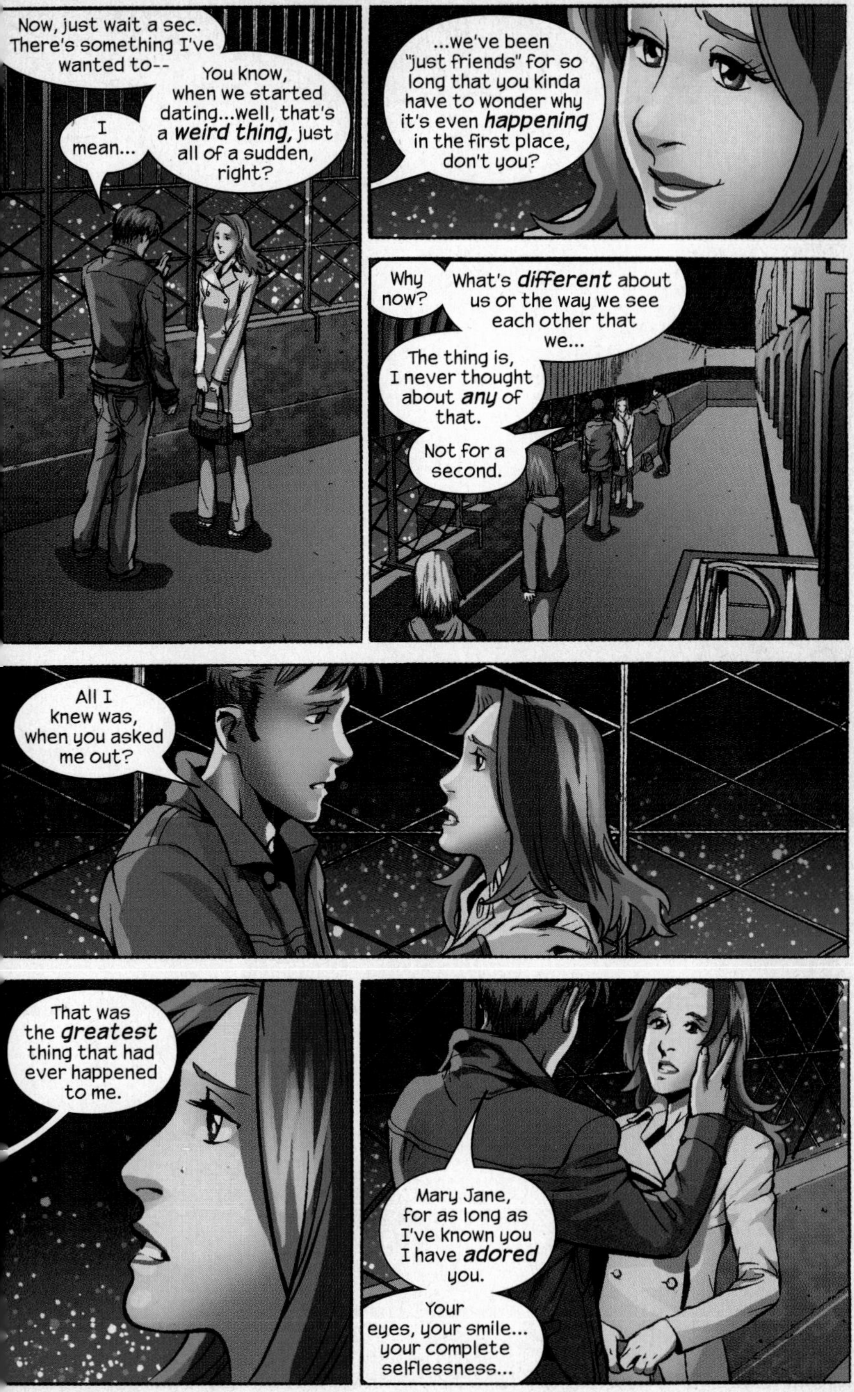

Now, just wait a sec. There's something I've wanted to--
I mean...
You know, when we started dating...well, that's a weird thing, just all of a sudden, right?
...we've been "just friends" for so long that you kinda have to wonder why it's even happening in the first place, don't you?
Why now?
What's different about us or the way we see each other that we...
The thing is, I never thought about any of that.
Not for a second.
All I knew was, when you asked me out?
That was the greatest thing that had ever happened to me.
Mary Jane, for as long as I've known you I have adored you.
Your eyes, your smile... your complete selflessness...

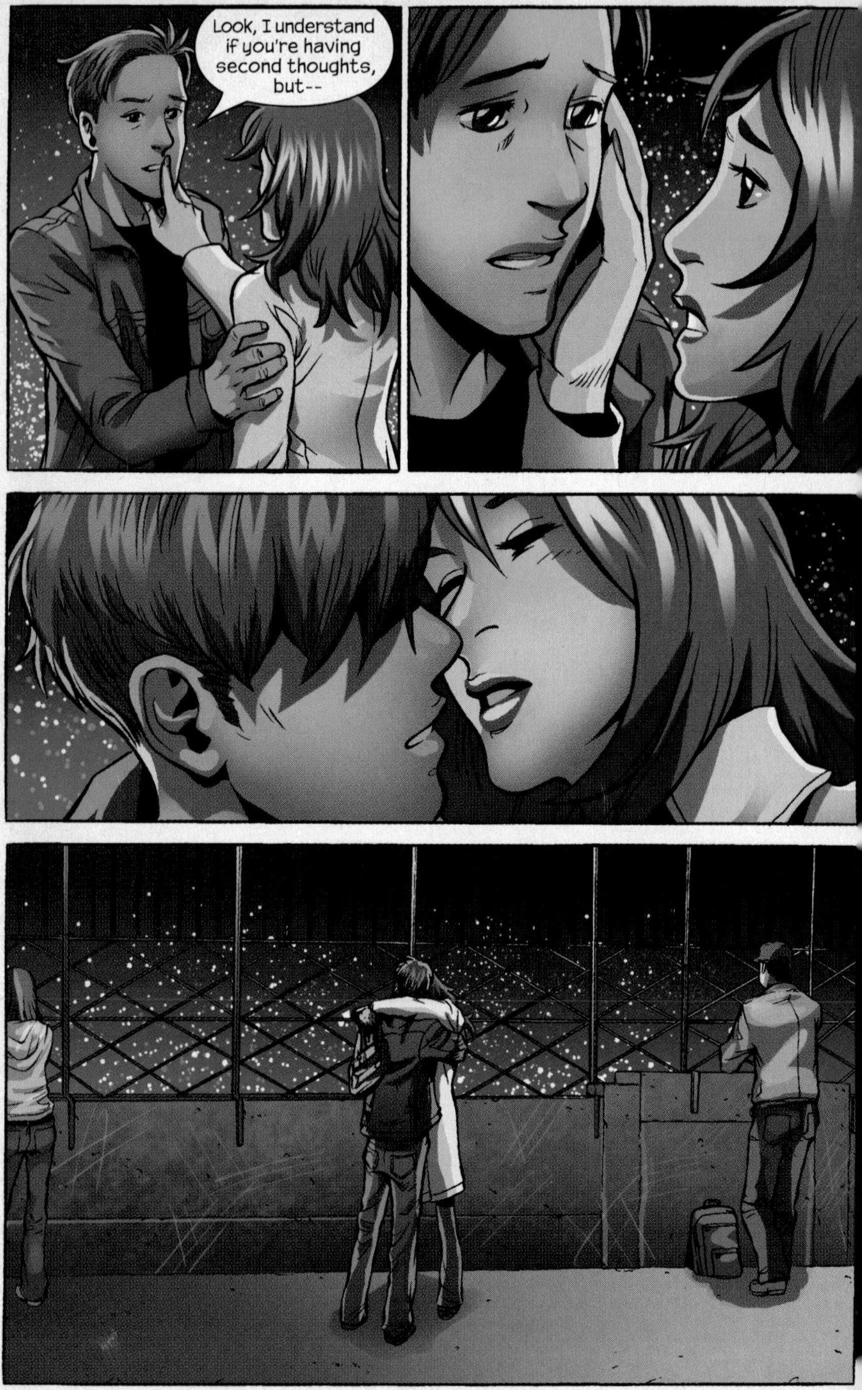
Look, I understand if you're having second thoughts, but--

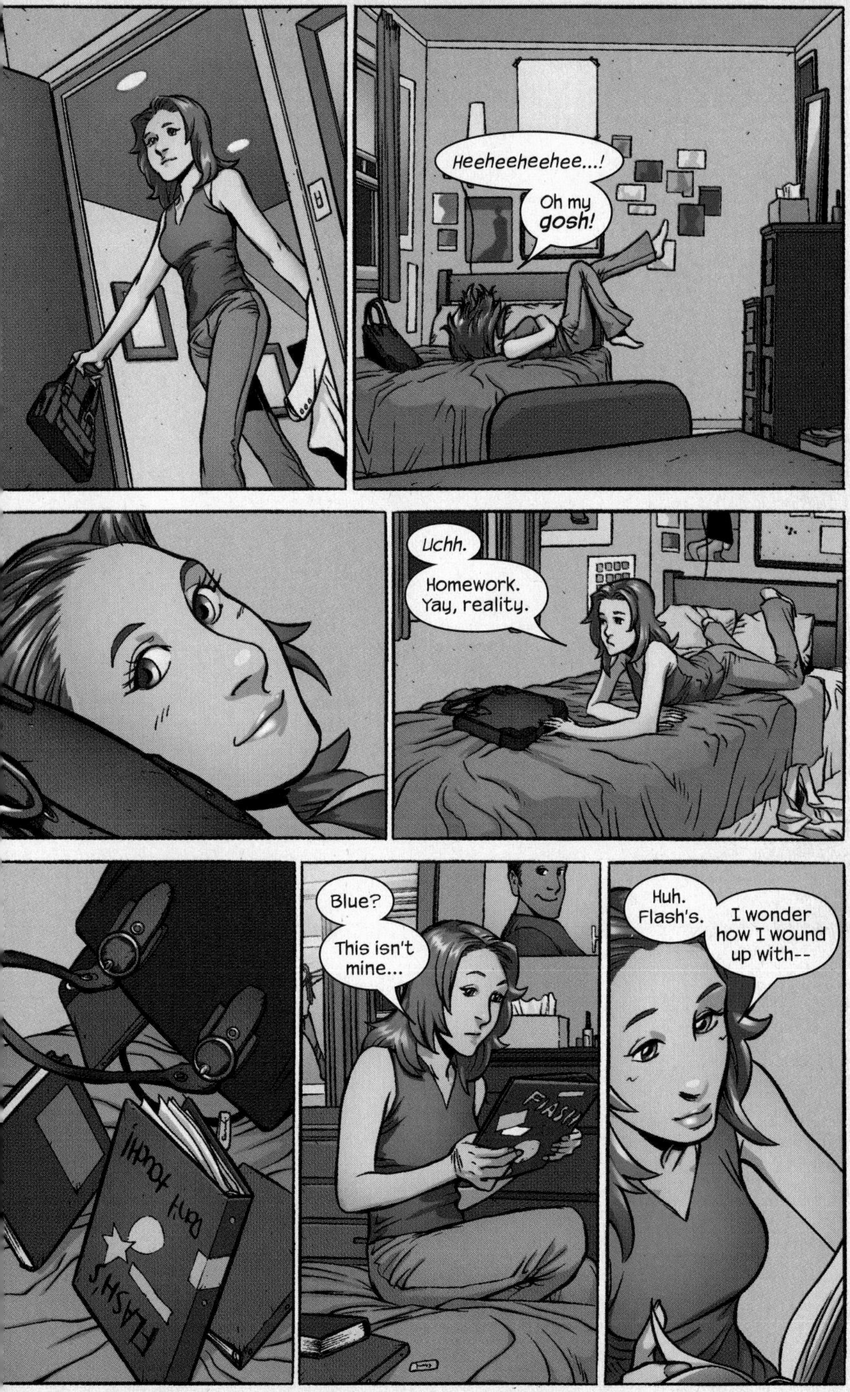
Heeheeheehee...!
Oh my gosh!
Uchh.
Homework. Yay, reality.
FLASH'S
Don't touch!!
Blue?
This isn't mine...
FLASH
Huh. Flash's.
I wonder how I wound up with--

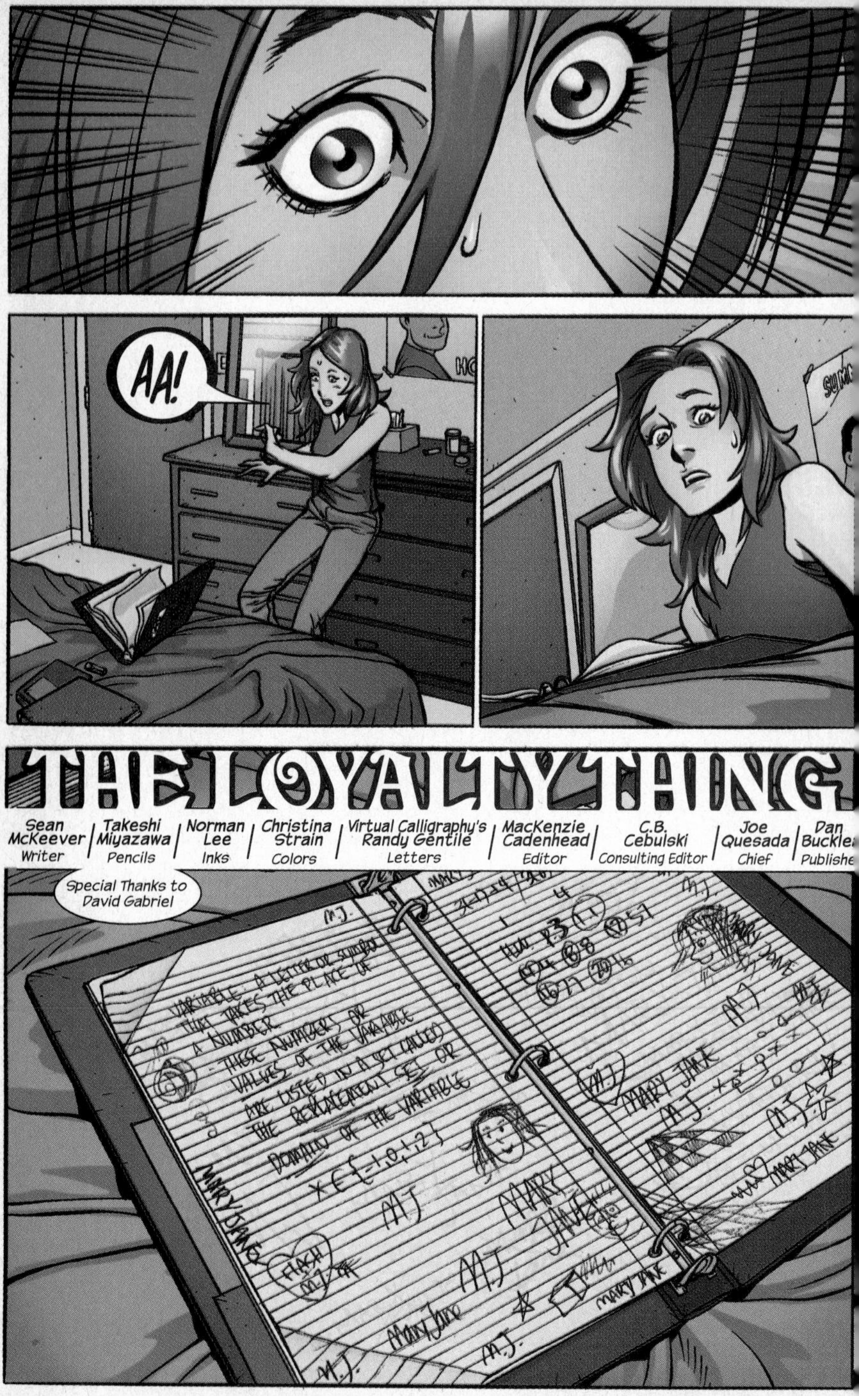
AA!
THE LOYALTY THING
Sean McKeever Writer
Takeshi Miyazawa Pencils
Norman Lee Inks
Christina Strain Colors
Virtual Calligraphy's Randy Gentile Letters
MacKenzie Cadenhead Editor
C.B. Cebulski Consulting Editor
Joe Quesada Chief
Dan Buckle[a] Publishe[r]
Special Thanks to David Gabriel

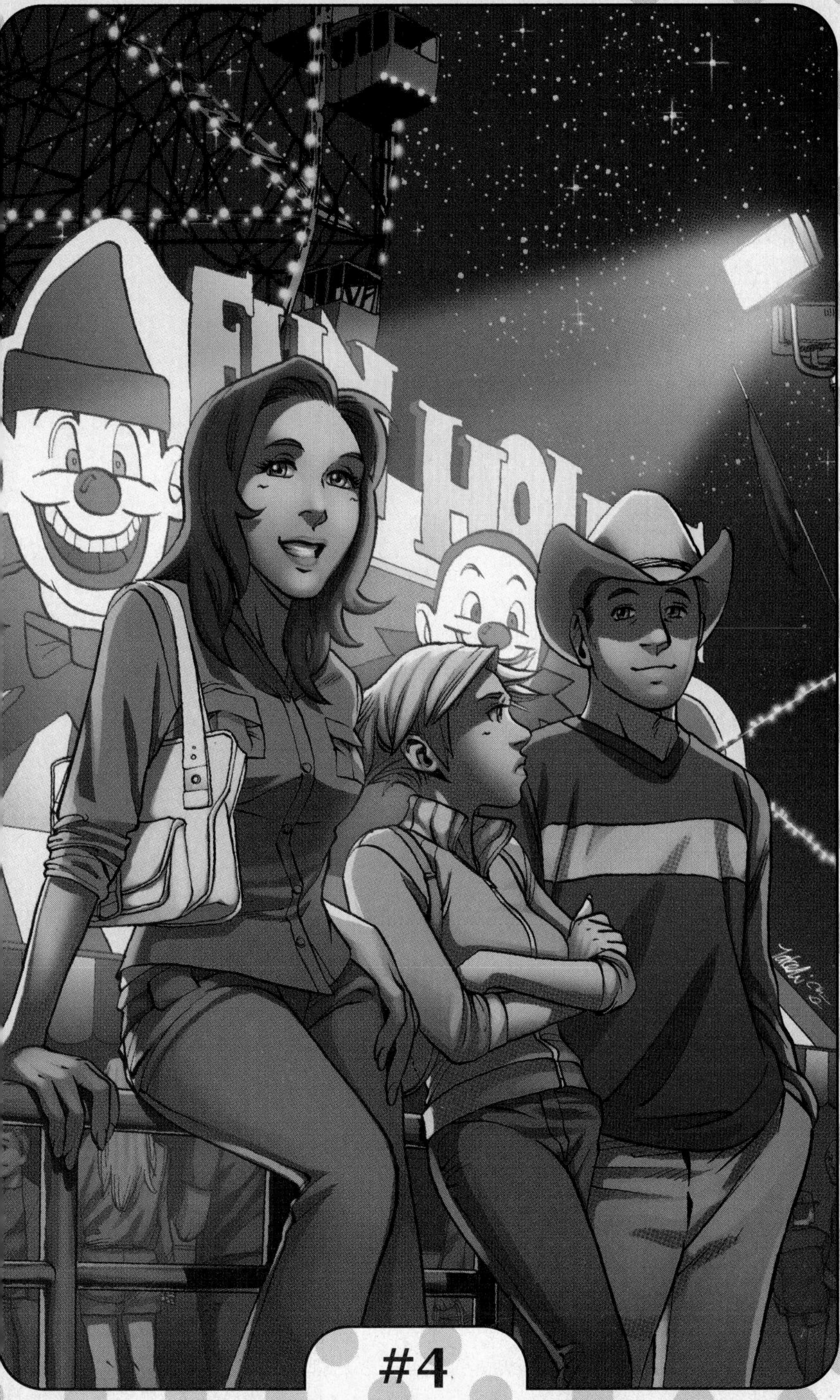

#4

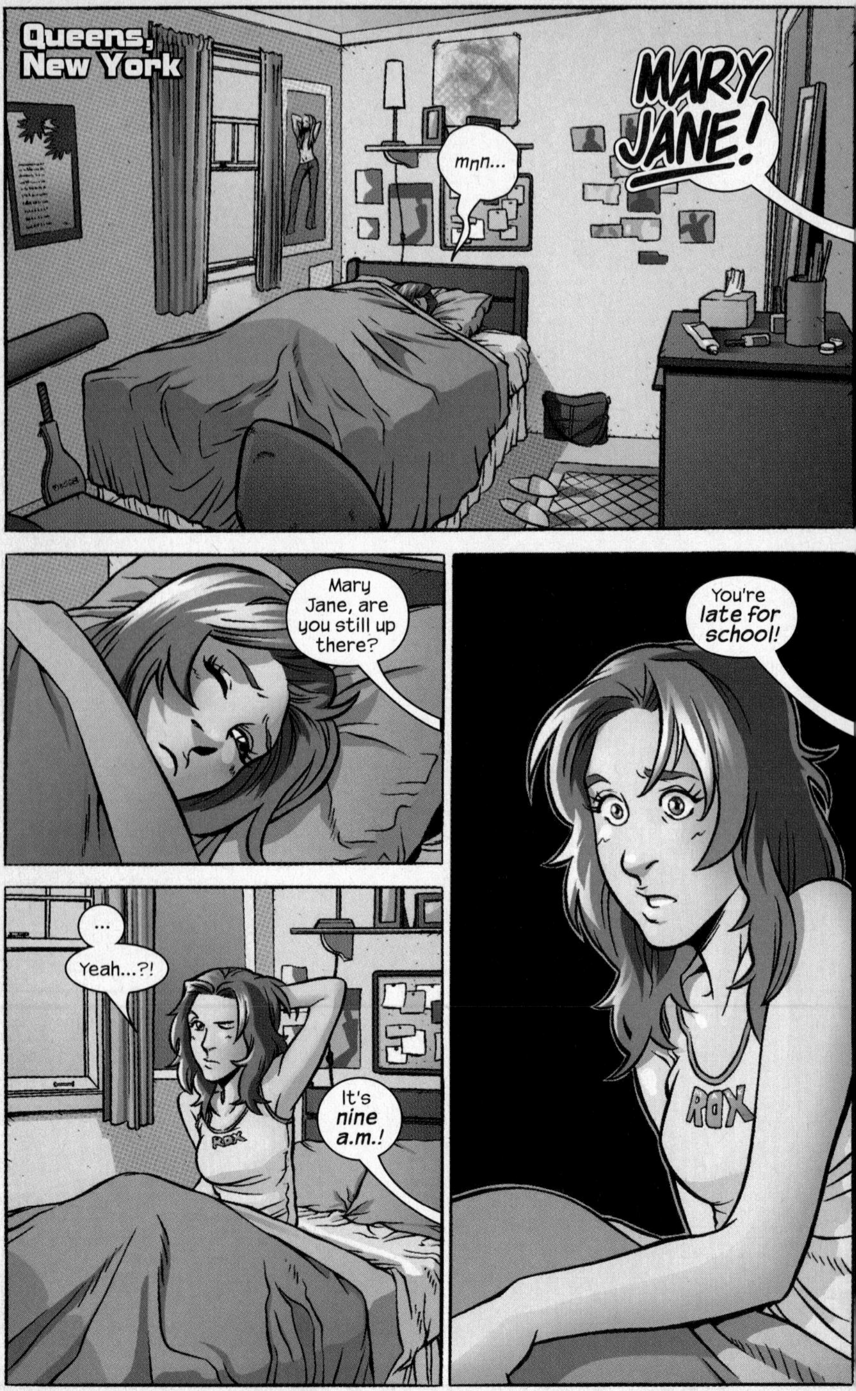
Queens, New York
MARY JANE!
mnn...
Mary Jane, are you still up there?
...
Yeah...?!
It's nine a.m.!
You're late for school!

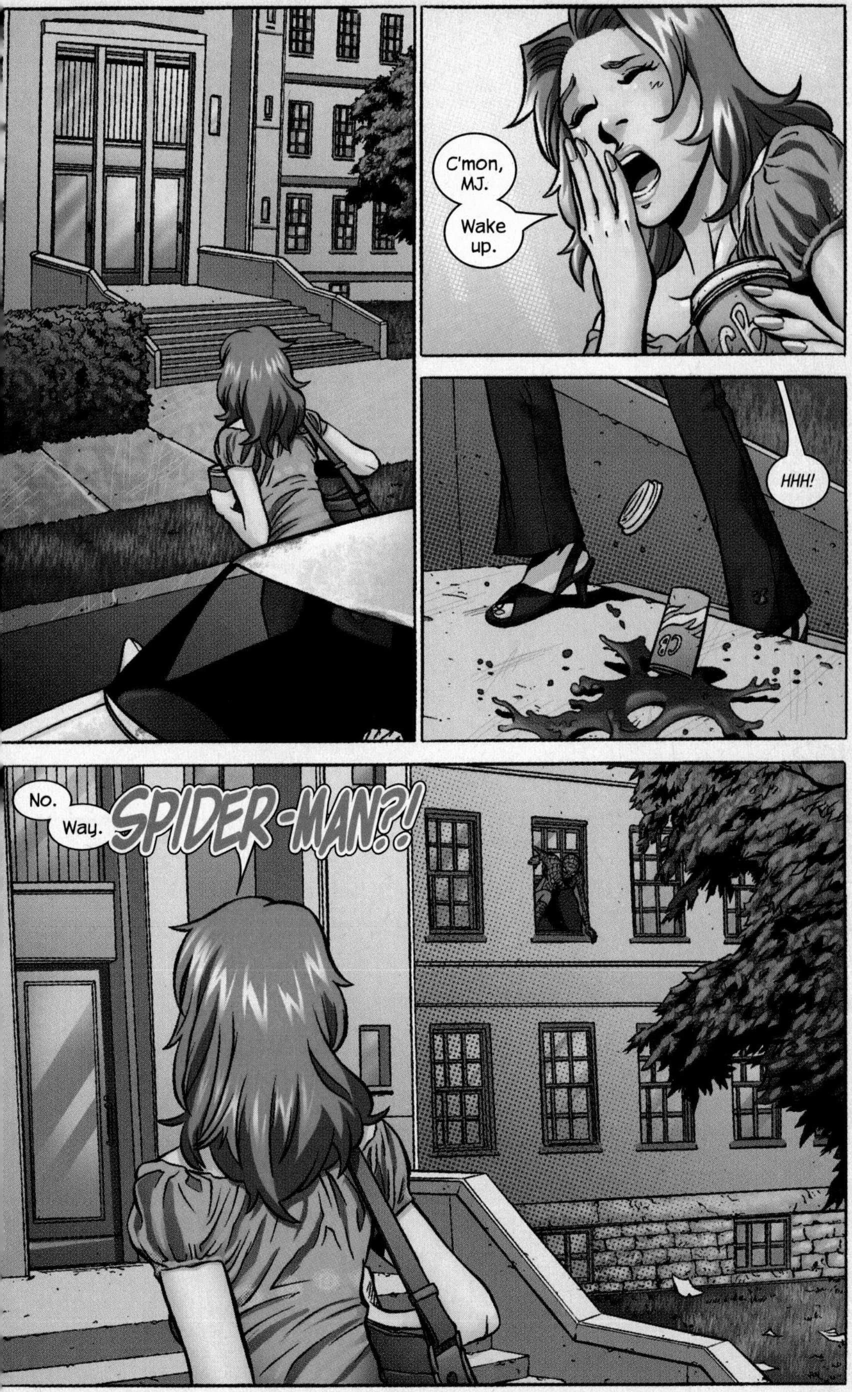
C'mon, MJ.
Wake up.
HHH!
No.
Way.
SPIDER-MAN?!

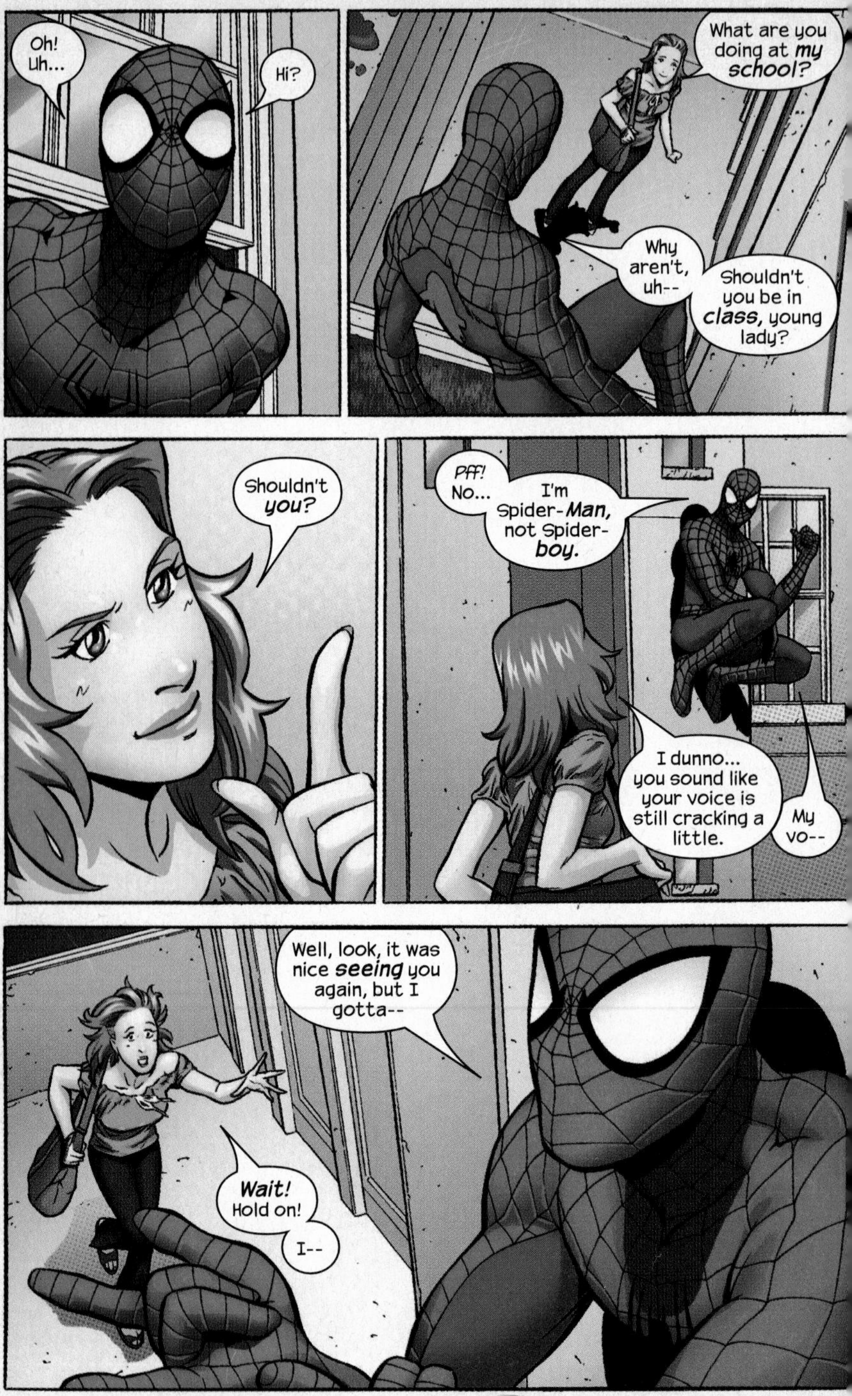
Oh! Uh...
Hi?
What are you doing at *my school?*
Why aren't, uh--
Shouldn't you be in *class,* young lady?
Shouldn't *you?*
Pff! No...
I'm Spider-*Man,* not Spider-*boy.*
I dunno... you sound like your voice is still cracking a little.
My vo--
Well, look, it was nice *seeing* you again, but I gotta--
Wait! Hold on!
I--

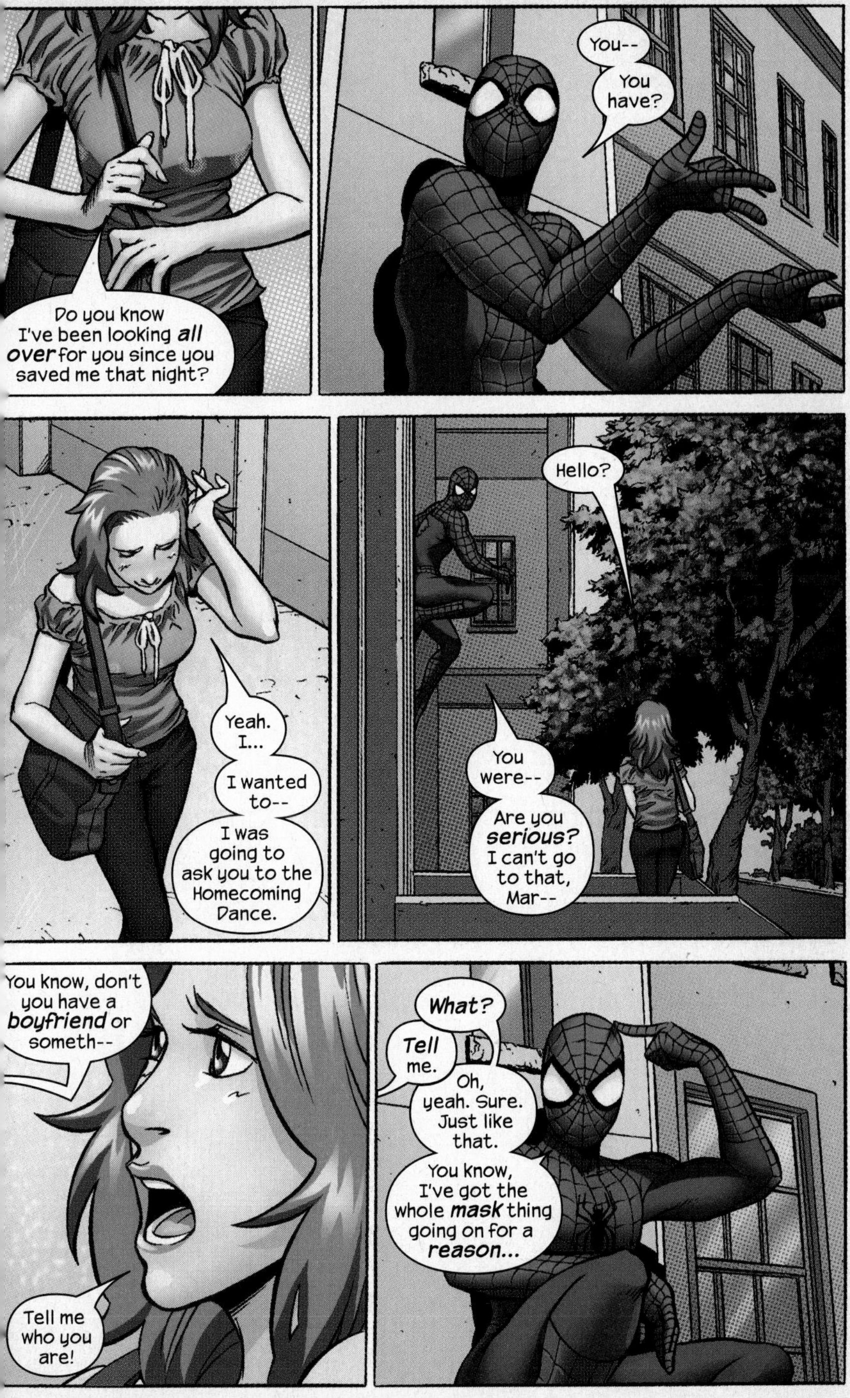
Do you know I've been looking *all over* for you since you saved me that night?
You--
You have?
Yeah. I...
I wanted to--
I was going to ask you to the Homecoming Dance.
Hello?
You were--
Are you *serious?* I can't go to that, Mar--
You know, don't you have a *boyfriend* or someth--
Tell me who you are!
What?
Tell me.
Oh, yeah. Sure. Just like that.
You know, I've got the whole *mask* thing going on for a *reason...*

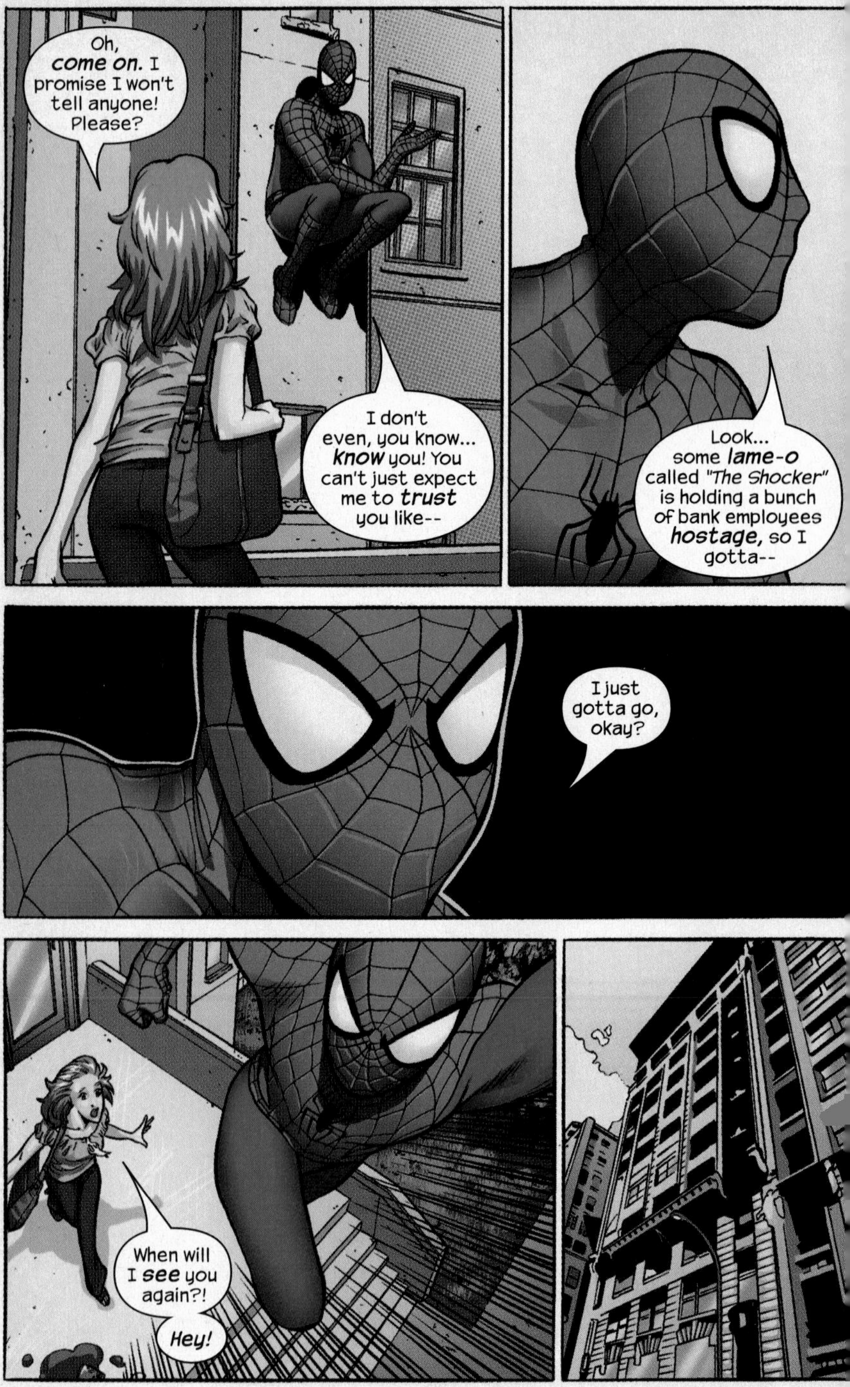

Oh, *come on.* I promise I won't tell anyone! Please?
I don't even, you know... *know* you! You can't just expect me to *trust* you like--
Look... some *lame-o* called *"The Shocker"* is holding a bunch of bank employees *hostage,* so I gotta--
I just gotta go, okay?
When will I *see* you again?!
Hey!

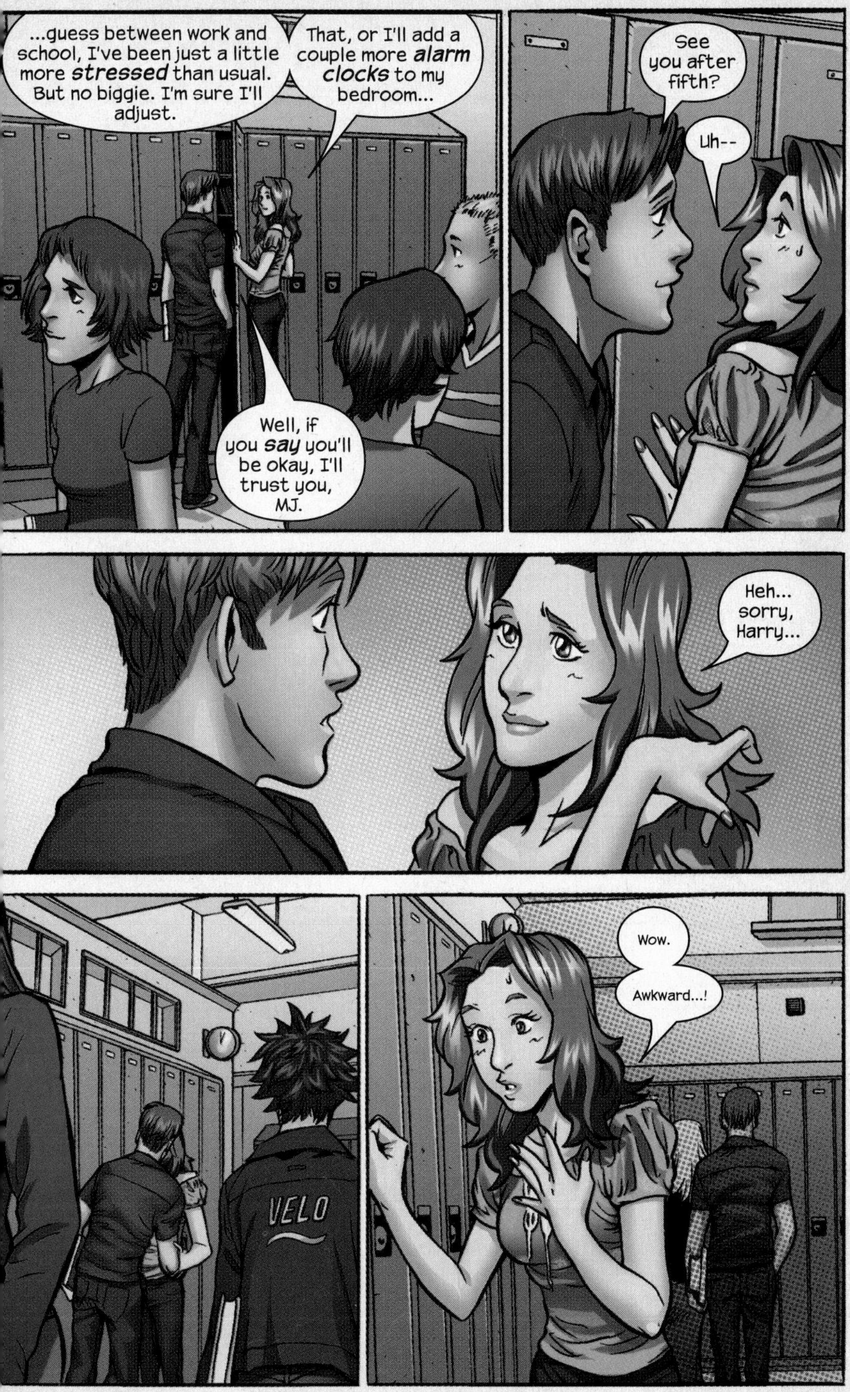
...guess between work and school, I've been just a little more *stressed* than usual. But no biggie. I'm sure I'll adjust.
That, or I'll add a couple more *alarm clocks* to my bedroom...
Well, if you *say* you'll be okay, I'll trust you, MJ.
See you after fifth?
Uh--
Heh... sorry, Harry...
VELO
Wow.
Awkward...!

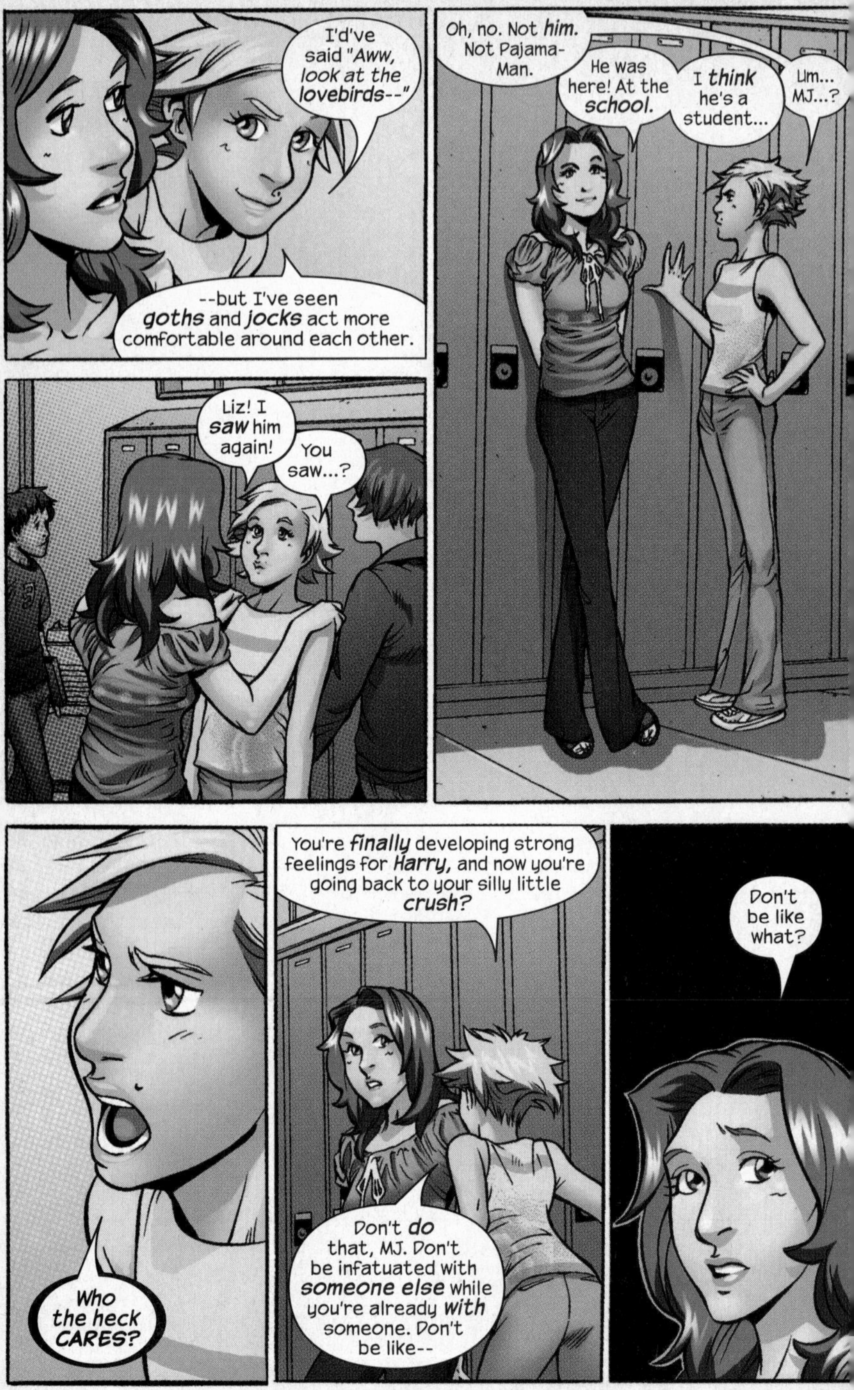
I'd've said "Aww, look at the lovebirds--"
--but I've seen goths and jocks act more comfortable around each other.
Liz! I saw him again!
You saw...?
Oh, no. Not him. Not Pajama-Man.
He was here! At the school.
I think he's a student...
Um... MJ...?
Who the heck CARES?
You're finally developing strong feelings for Harry, and now you're going back to your silly little crush?
Don't do that, MJ. Don't be infatuated with someone else while you're already with someone. Don't be like--
Don't be like what?

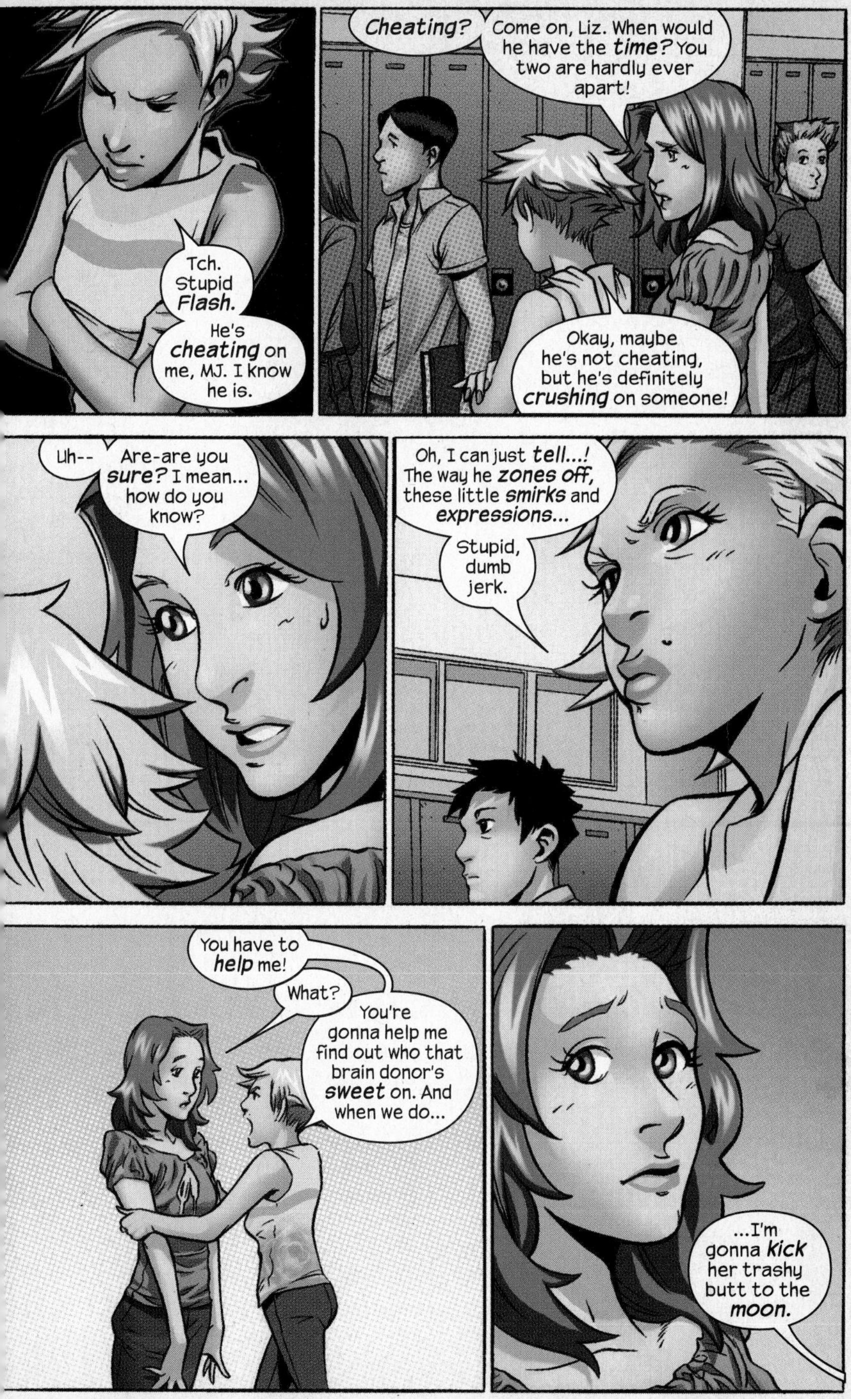
Tch. Stupid *Flash.*
He's *cheating* on me, MJ. I know he is.
Cheating?
Come on, Liz. When would he have the *time?* You two are hardly ever apart!
Okay, maybe he's not cheating, but he's definitely *crushing* on someone!
Uh--
Are-are you *sure?* I mean... how do you know?
Oh, I can just *tell...!* The way he *zones off,* these little *smirks* and *expressions...*
Stupid, dumb jerk.
You have to *help* me!
What?
You're gonna help me find out who that brain donor's *sweet* on. And when we do...
...I'm gonna *kick* her trashy butt to the *moon.*

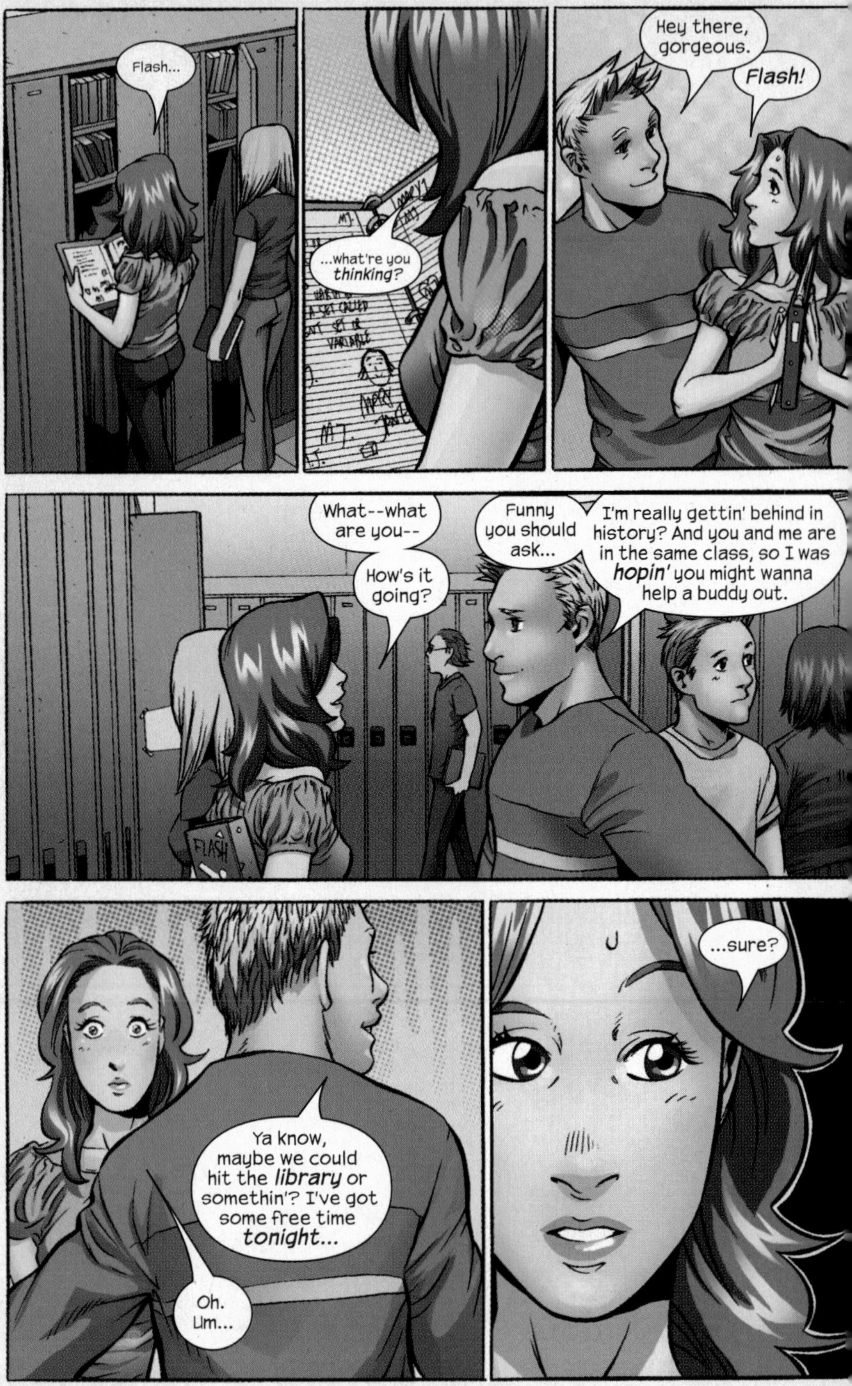
Flash...
...what're you *thinking*?
Hey there, gorgeous.
Flash!
What--what are you--
How's it going?
Funny you should ask...
I'm really gettin' behind in history? And you and me are in the same class, so I was *hopin'* you might wanna help a buddy out.
Ya know, maybe we could hit the *library* or somethin'? I've got some free time *tonight...*
Oh. Um...
...sure?

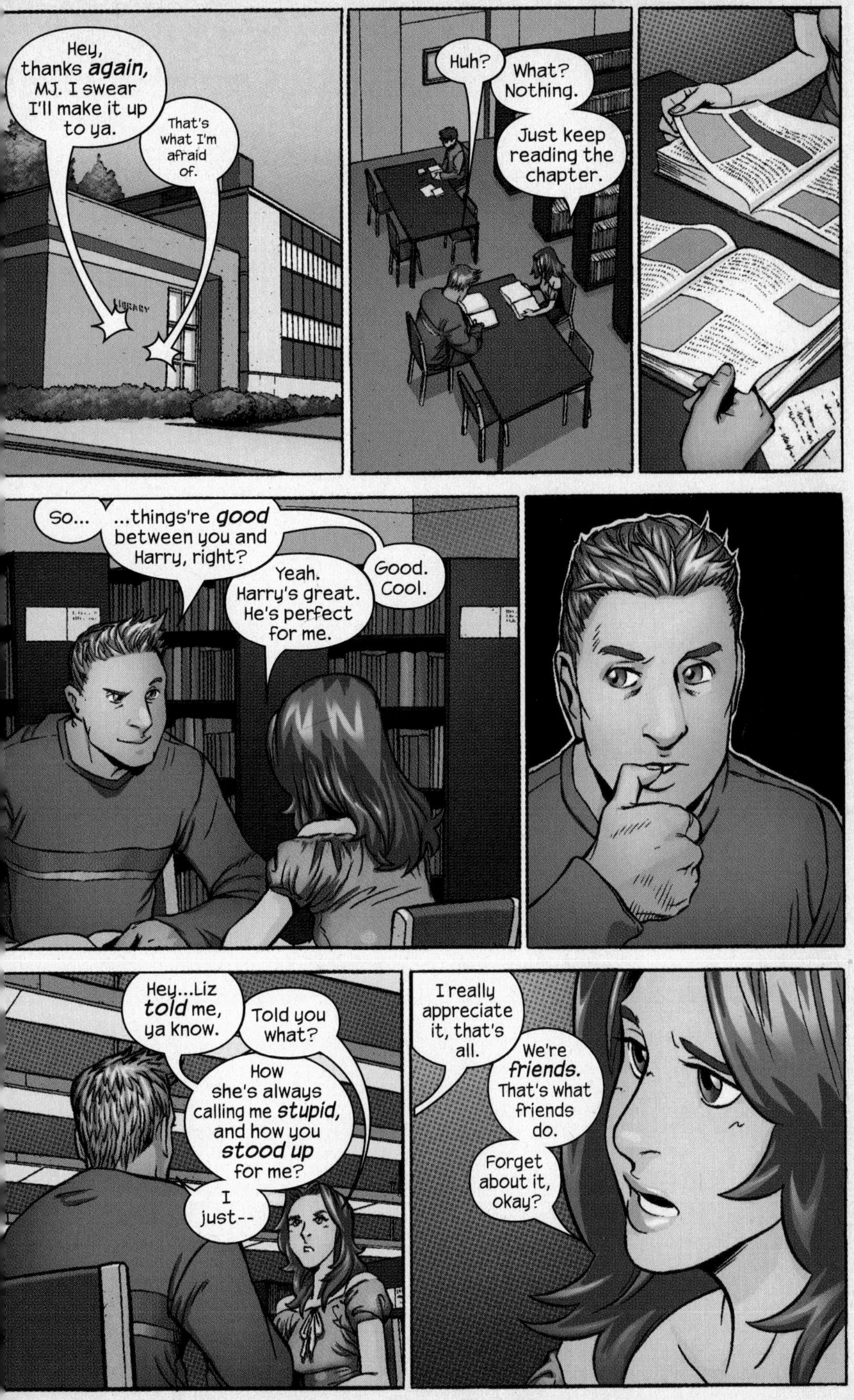
Hey, thanks again, MJ. I swear I'll make it up to ya.
That's what I'm afraid of.
LIBRARY
Huh?
What? Nothing.
Just keep reading the chapter.
So...
...things're good between you and Harry, right?
Yeah. Harry's great. He's perfect for me.
Good. Cool.
Hey...Liz told me, ya know.
Told you what?
How she's always calling me stupid, and how you stood up for me?
I just--
I really appreciate it, that's all.
We're friends. That's what friends do.
Forget about it, okay?

'Cause, ya know, I don't think she *sees* me the same way you do.

I mean...I don't really think *anybody* does.

Do you ever wonder if--

Flash?

Yeah?

Keep reading.

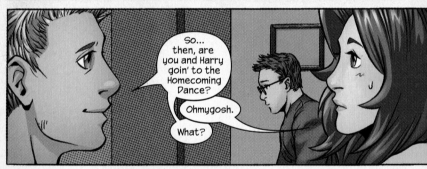

So... then, are you and Harry goin' to the Homecoming Dance?

Ohmygosh.

What?

You know what? I forgot. I totally forgot.

I have to meet my mom for this *thing*, and...and I'm *totally late* now.

Gotta go.

Uh...see ya?

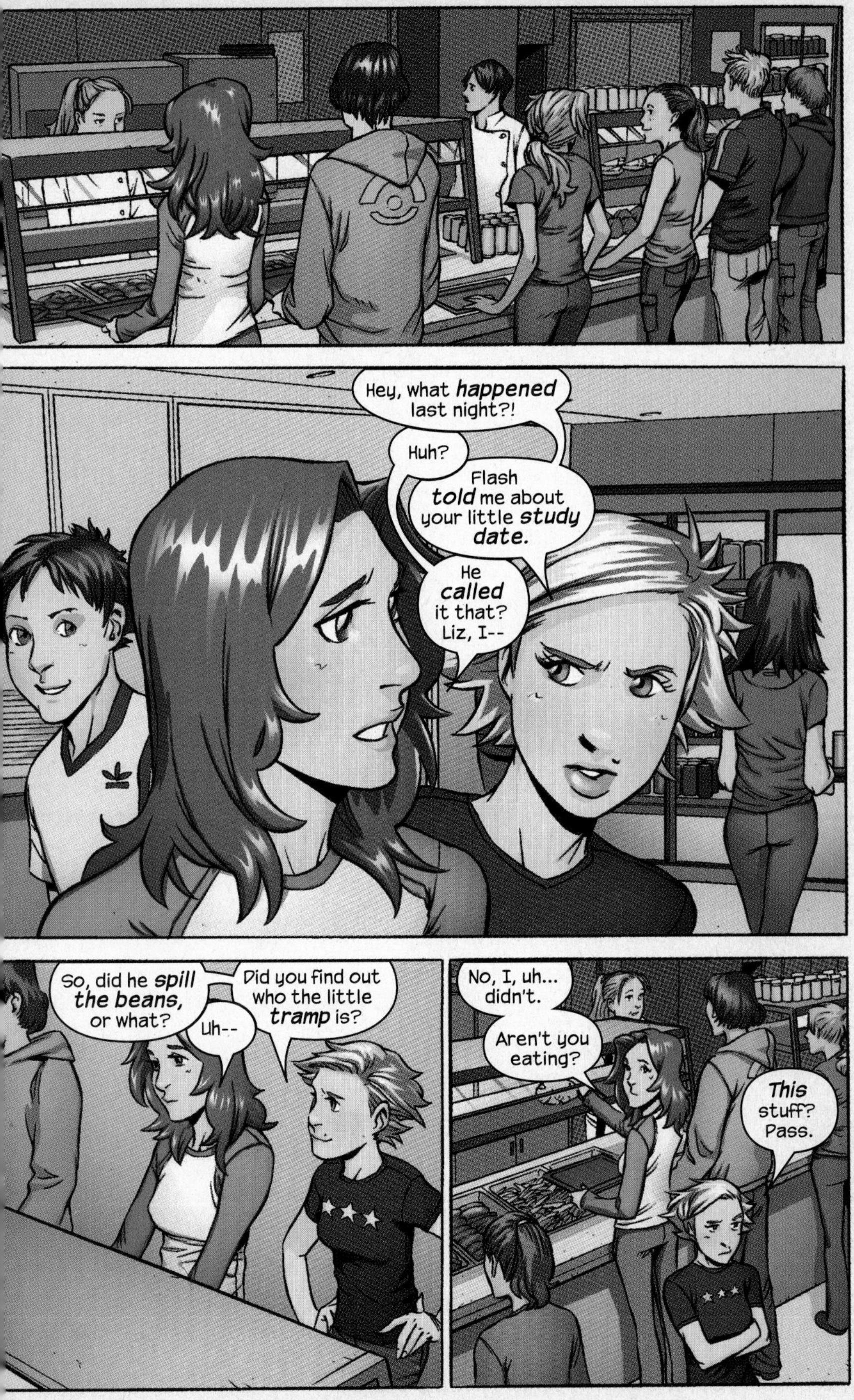
Hey, what happened last night?!
Huh?
Flash told me about your little study date.
He called it that? Liz, I--
So, did he spill the beans, or what?
Uh--
Did you find out who the little tramp is?
No, I, uh... didn't.
Aren't you eating?
This stuff? Pass.

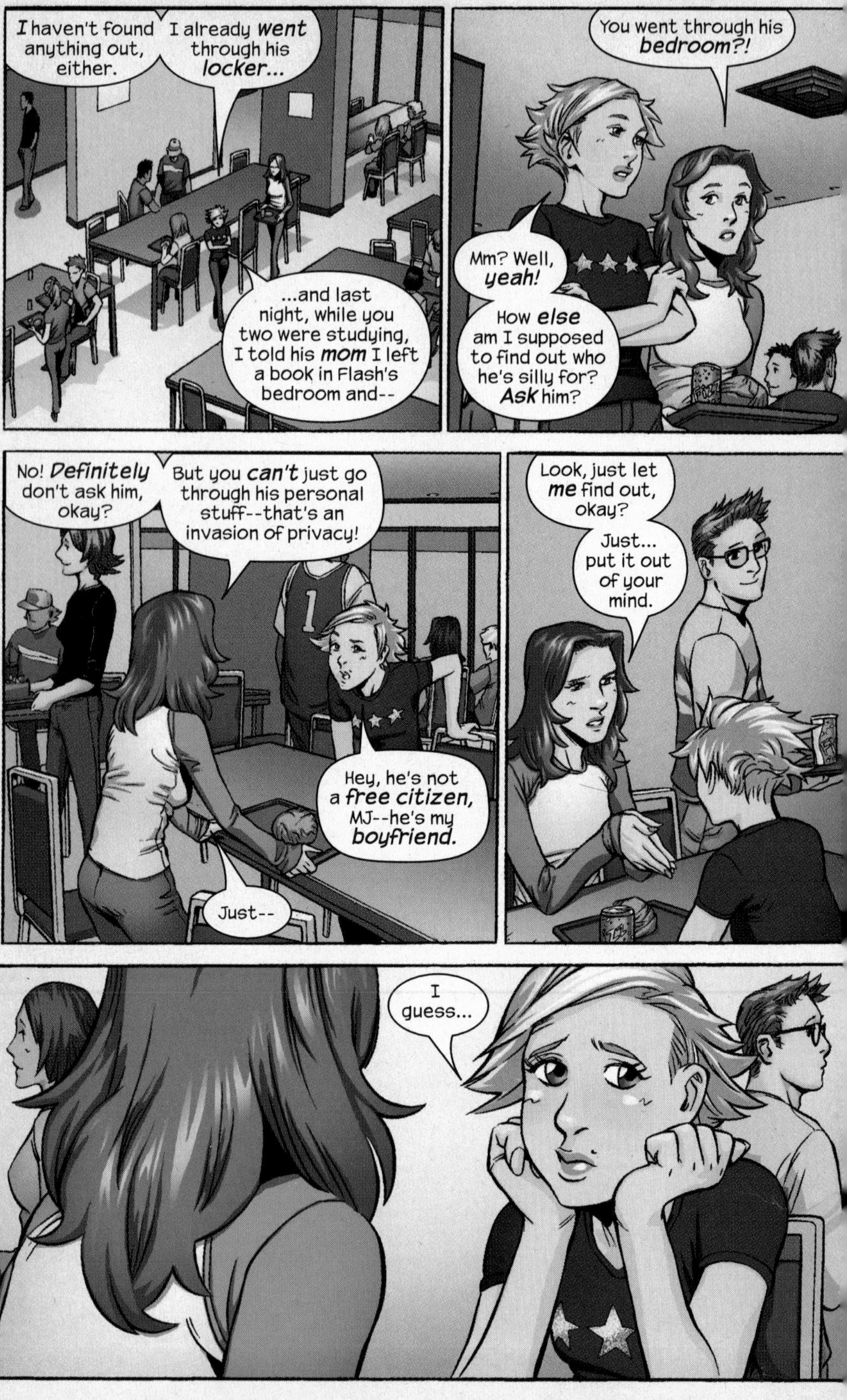
I haven't found anything out, either.
I already went through his locker...
...and last night, while you two were studying, I told his mom I left a book in Flash's bedroom and--
You went through his bedroom?!
Mm? Well, yeah!
How else am I supposed to find out who he's silly for? Ask him?
No! Definitely don't ask him, okay?
But you can't just go through his personal stuff--that's an invasion of privacy!
Hey, he's not a free citizen, MJ--he's my boyfriend.
Just--
Look, just let me find out, okay?
Just... put it out of your mind.
I guess...

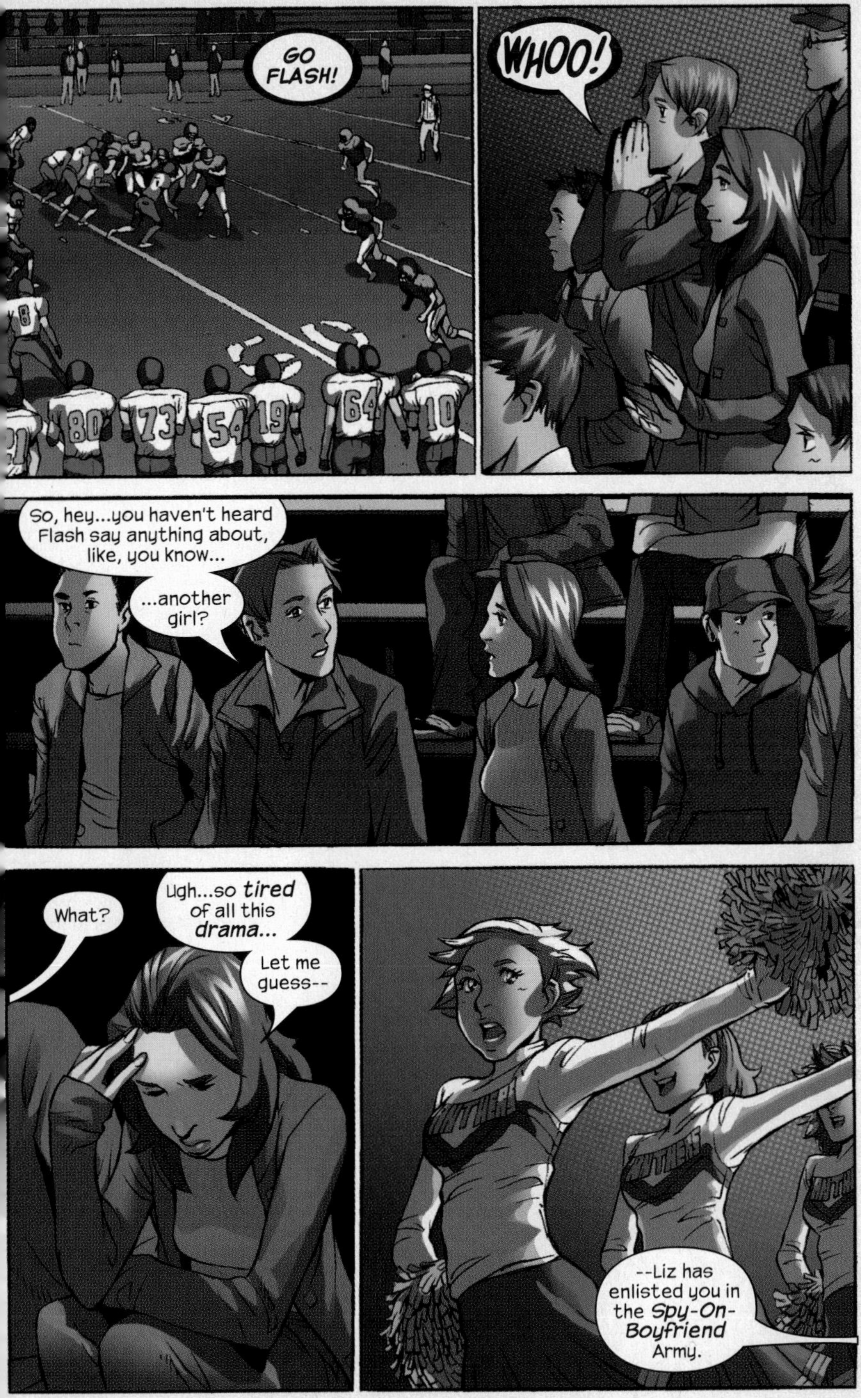
GO FLASH!
WHOO!
So, hey...you haven't heard Flash say anything about, like, you know...
...another girl?
What?
Ugh...so *tired* of all this *drama...*
Let me guess--
--Liz has enlisted you in the *Spy-On-Boyfriend* Army.

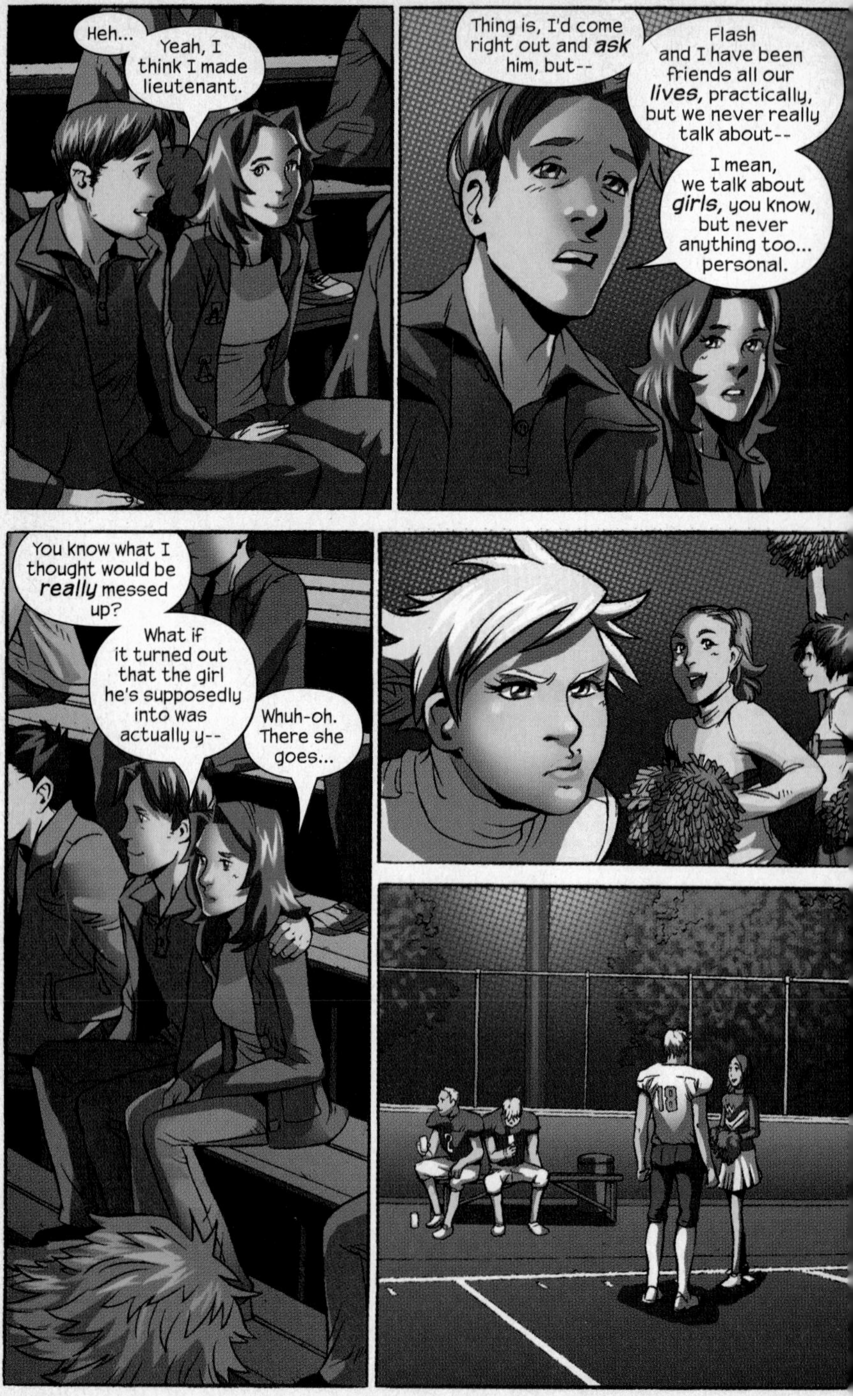
Heh...
Yeah, I think I made lieutenant.
Thing is, I'd come right out and ask him, but--
Flash and I have been friends all our lives, practically, but we never really talk about--
I mean, we talk about girls, you know, but never anything too... personal.
You know what I thought would be really messed up?
What if it turned out that the girl he's supposedly into was actually y--
Whuh-oh. There she goes...

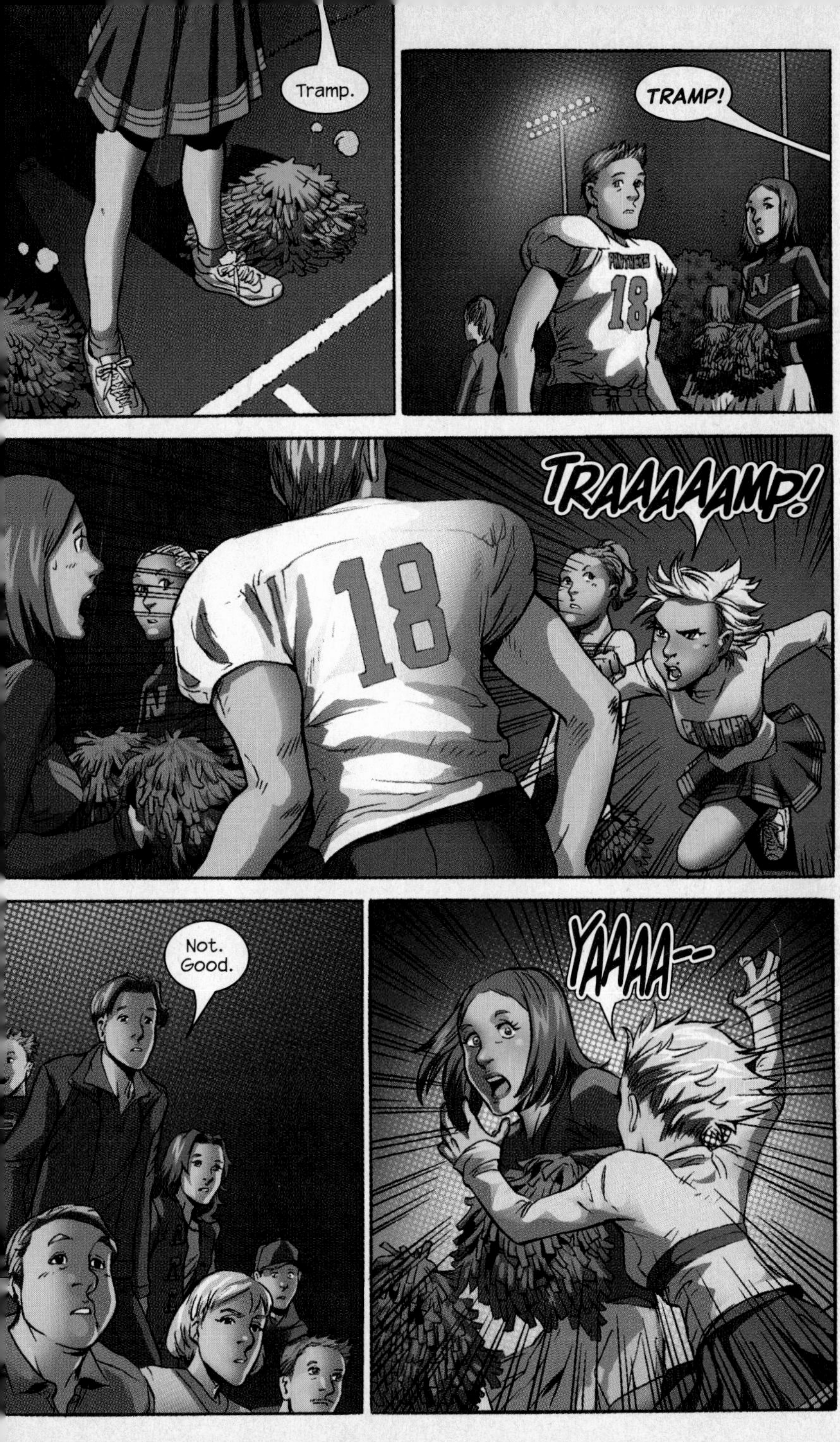
Tramp.
TRAMP!
TRAAAAAMP!
Not. Good.
YAAAA--

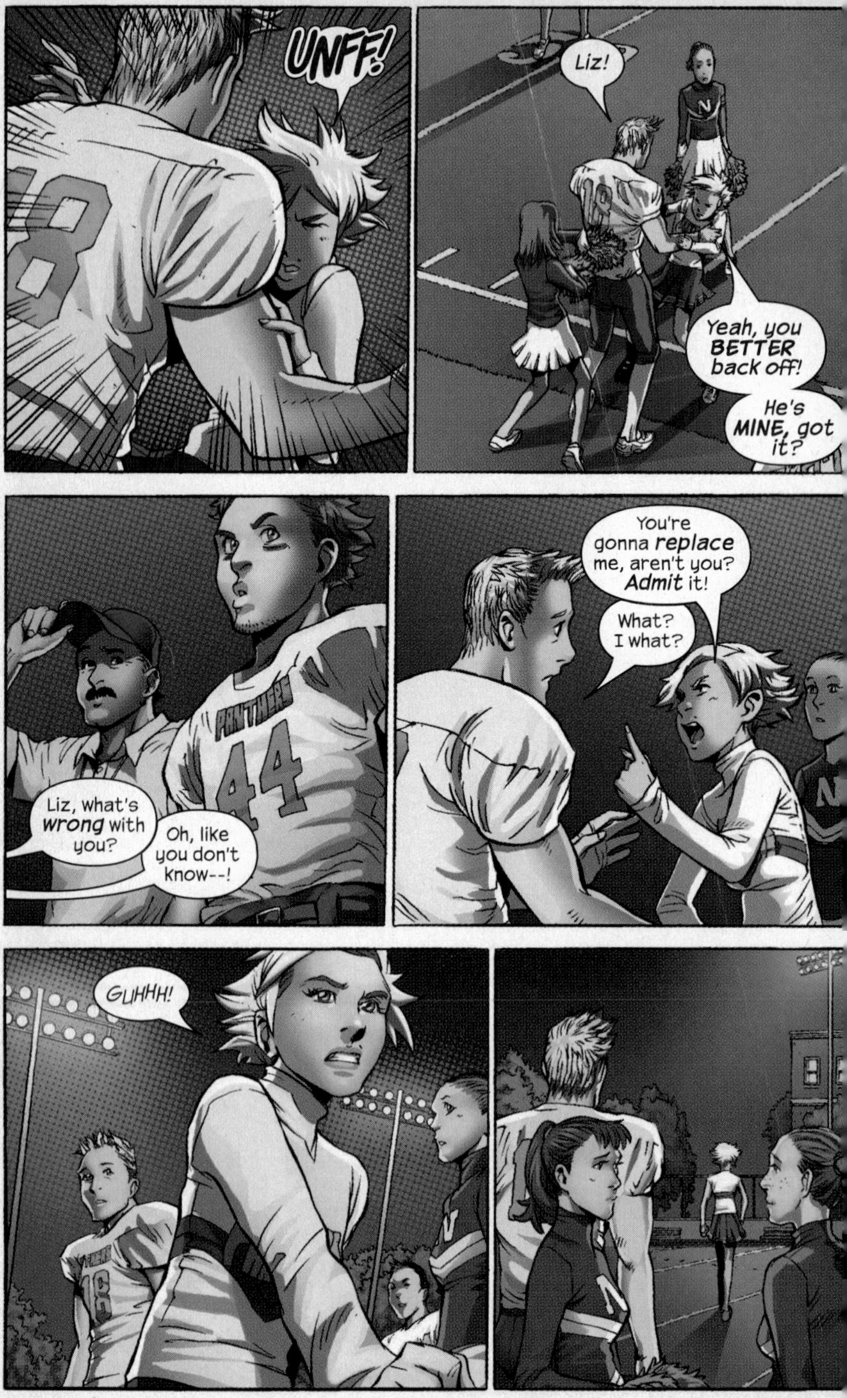
UNFF!
Liz!
Yeah, you BETTER back off!
He's MINE, got it?
Liz, what's wrong with you?
Oh, like you don't know--!
You're gonna replace me, aren't you? Admit it!
What? I what?
GUHHH!
PANTHERS
44

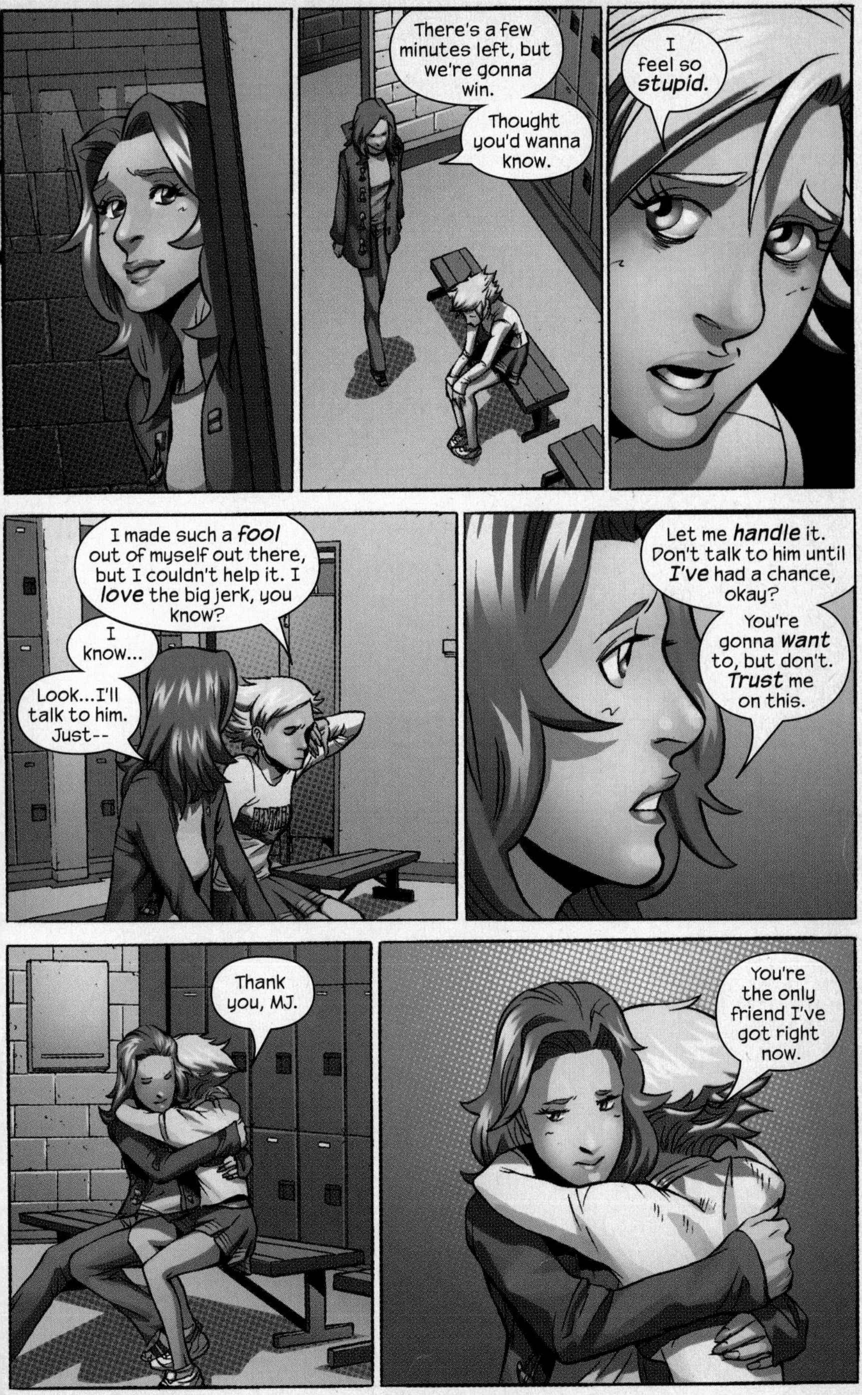
There's a few minutes left, but we're gonna win.
Thought you'd wanna know.
I feel so *stupid.*
I made such a *fool* out of myself out there, but I couldn't help it. I *love* the big jerk, you know?
I know...
Look...I'll talk to him. Just--
Let me *handle* it. Don't talk to him until *I've* had a chance, okay?
You're gonna *want* to, but don't. *Trust* me on this.
Thank you, MJ.
You're the only friend I've got right now.

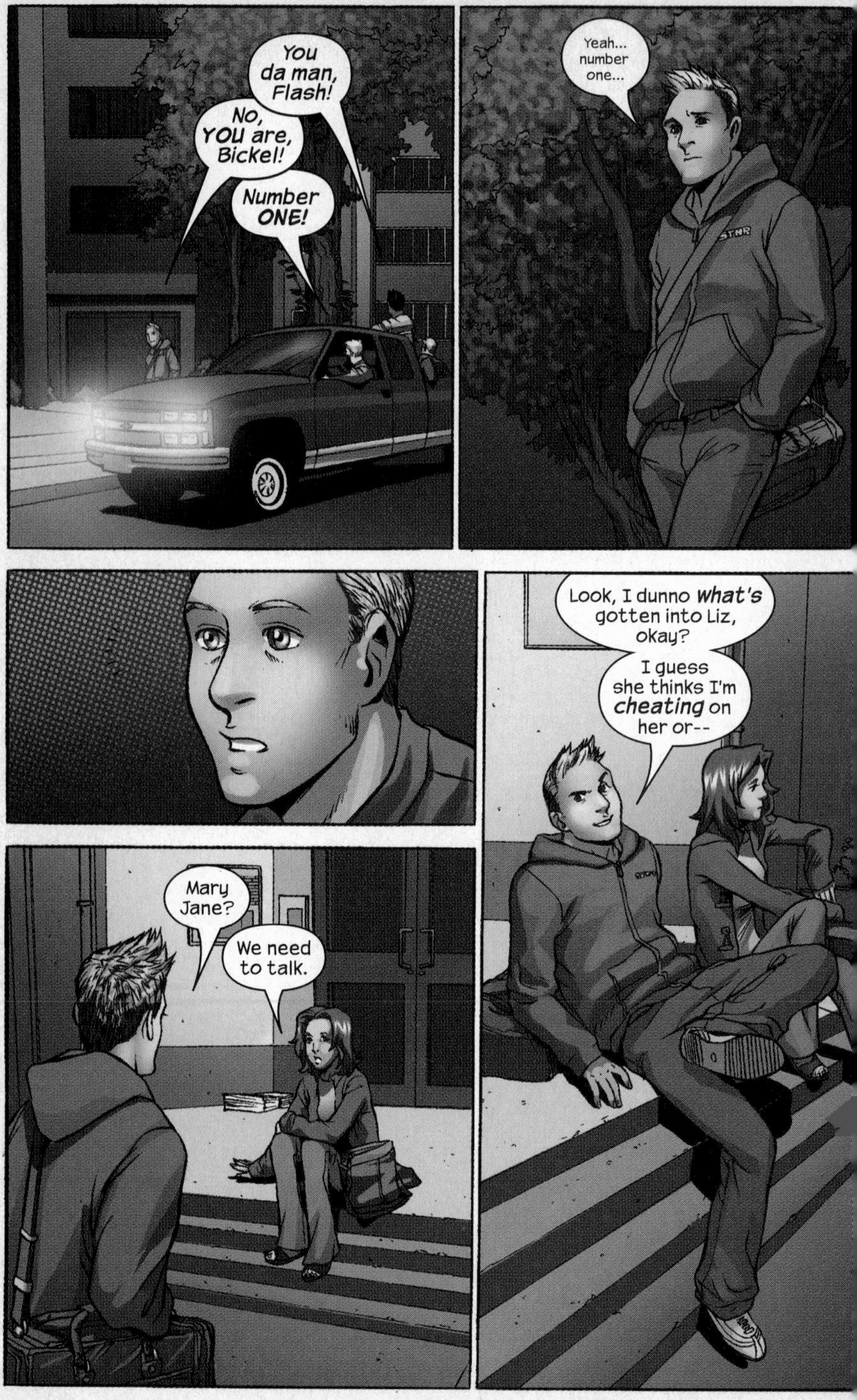
You da man, Flash!
No, YOU are, Bickel!
Number ONE!
Yeah... number one...
Mary Jane?
We need to talk.
Look, I dunno what's gotten into Liz, okay?
I guess she thinks I'm cheating on her or--

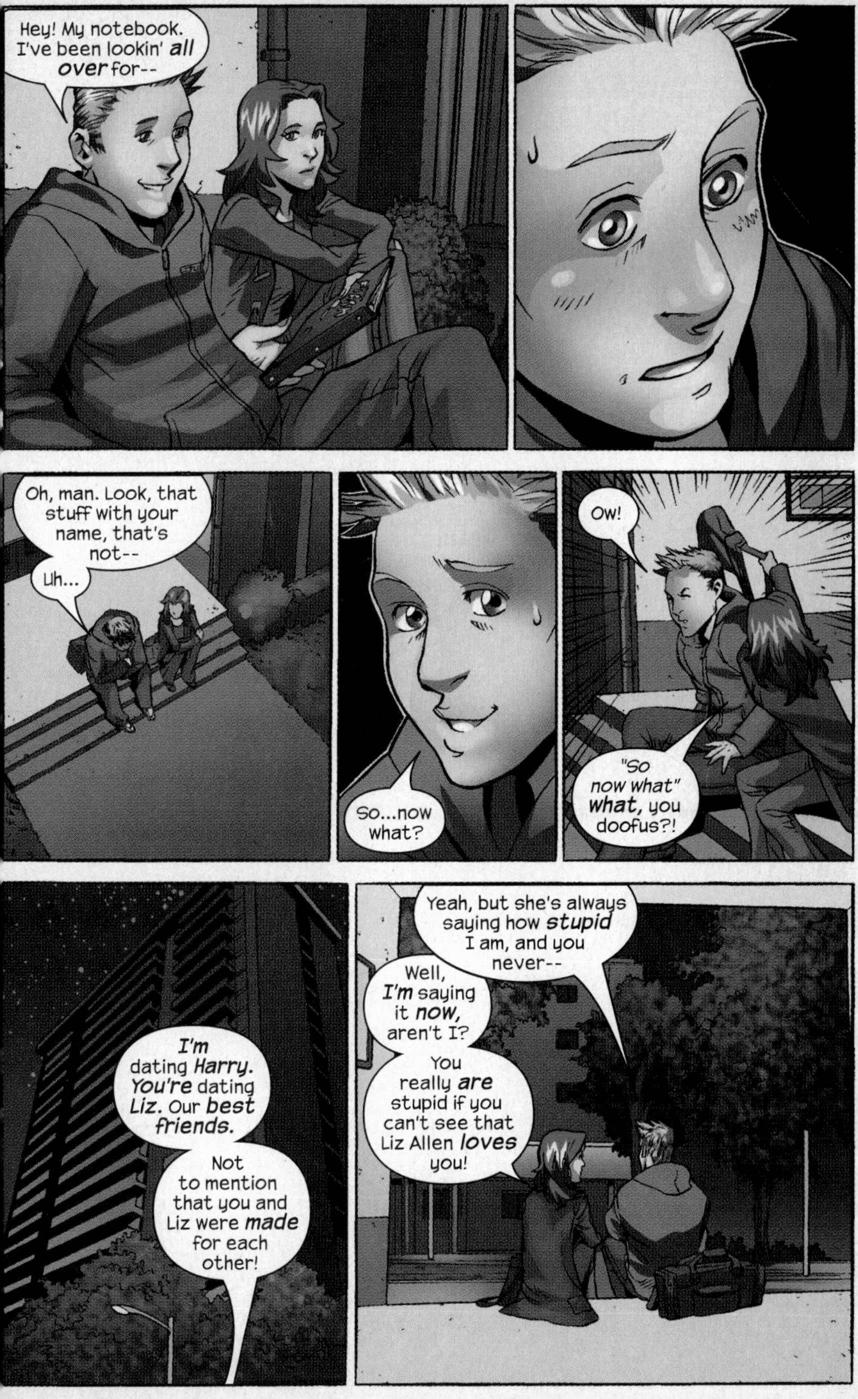
Hey! My notebook. I've been lookin' *all over* for--
Oh, man. Look, that stuff with your name, that's not--
Uh...
So...now what?
Ow!
"So now what" *what*, you doofus?!
I'm dating *Harry*. *You're* dating *Liz*. Our *best friends*.
Not to mention that you and Liz were *made* for each other!
Yeah, but she's always saying how *stupid* I am, and you never--
Well, *I'm* saying it *now*, aren't I?
You really *are* stupid if you can't see that Liz Allen *loves* you!

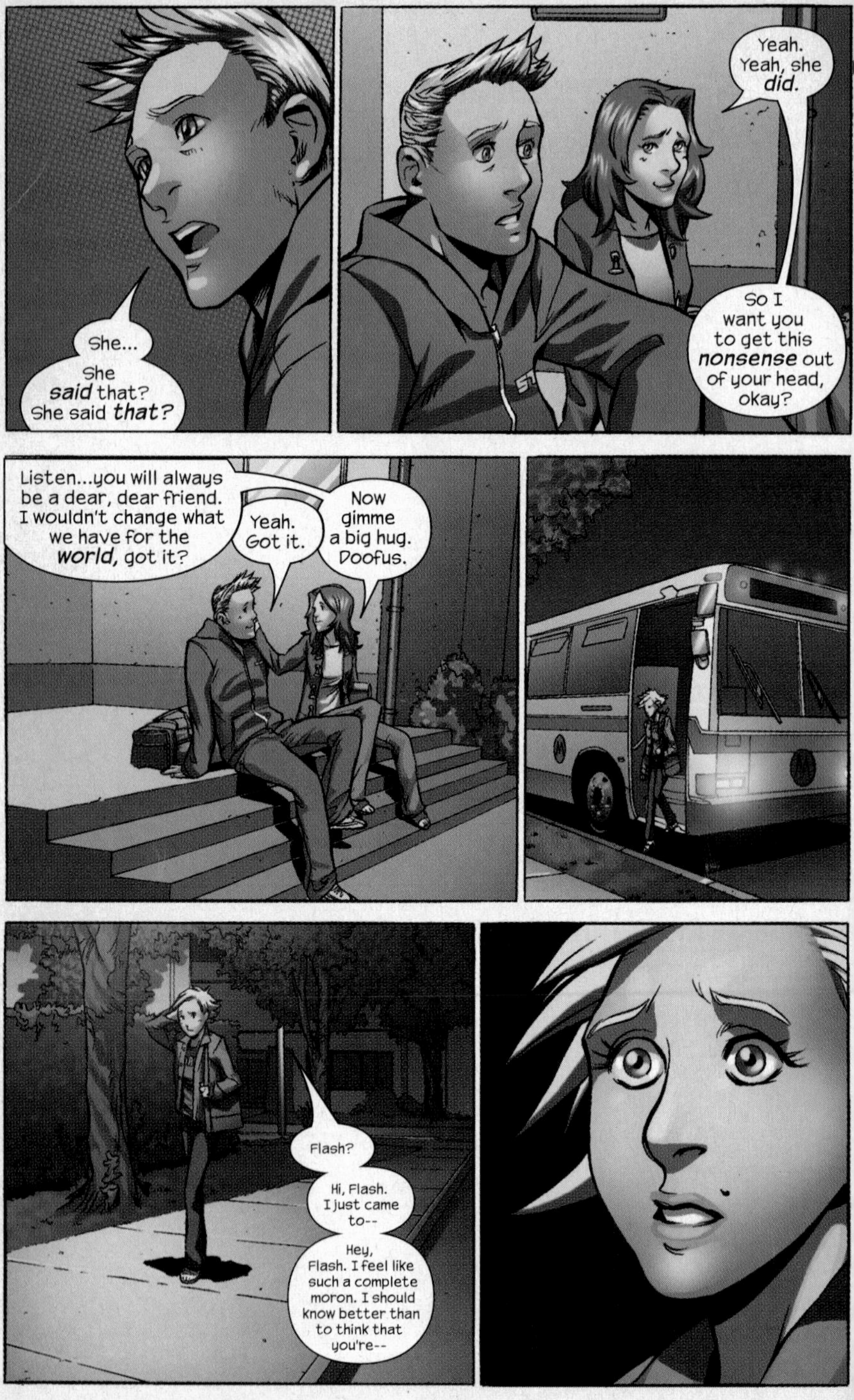
She...
She said that? She said that?
Yeah. Yeah, she did.
So I want you to get this nonsense out of your head, okay?
Listen...you will always be a dear, dear friend. I wouldn't change what we have for the world, got it?
Yeah. Got it.
Now gimme a big hug. Doofus.
Flash?
Hi, Flash. I just came to--
Hey, Flash. I feel like such a complete moron. I should know better than to think that you're--

THE TRUST THING

Sean McKeever | Takeshi Miyazawa | Norman Lee | Christina Strain
Writer | Pencils | inks | Colors

VC's Randy Gentile | MacKenzie Cadenhead | C.B. Cebulski
Letters | Editor | Consulting Editor

Joe Quesada | Dan Buckley | Special Thanks to David Gabriel
chief | Publisher

Team MJ

Sean McKeever - Writer

Born and raised in Wisconsin, writer Sean McKeever first made waves in the comics biz with his Indie teen drama, THE WAITING PLACE. He has since gone on to realize his dream job of writing for Marvel Comics, with such titles under his belt as SENTINEL, INHUMANS, THE INCREDIBLE HULK, SPIDER-GIRL and MYSTIQUE. Feel free to visit the big nerd himself at seanmckeever.com.

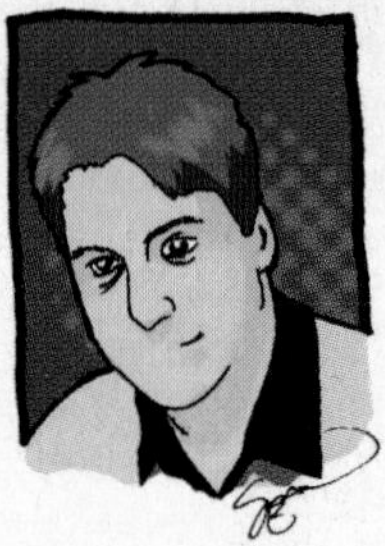

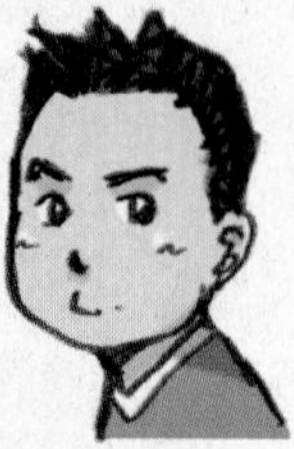

Takeshi Miyazawa - Penciler

A Canadian born and raised in Toronto, Canada. He went to school at Queen's University in Kingston Ontario for fine art and had aspirations of becoming a painter. He's still working on that dream but, for now, spends most of his time drawing and listening to CBC radio. He's never seen a UFO but would like to and likes eating pizza crust first.

Norman Lee - Inker

Norman is an Aquarius, enjoys theater, and long walks on the beach...Ooh sorry. Wrong bio. Located in Boston, MA with a degree in fashion illustration, Norman got into comics inking a WOLVERINE annual, DEADPOOL, then for various companies. (Dark Horse, DC, Disney). Besides inking, Norman plans on one day taking over the world and possibly making a spinach quiche.

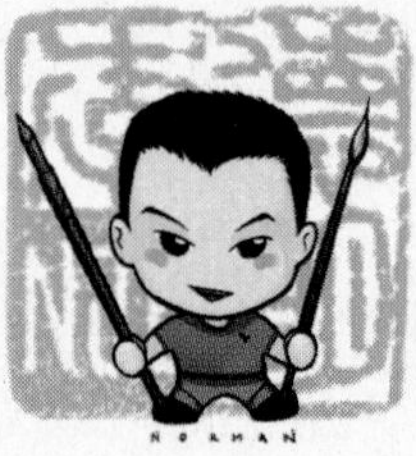
NORMAN

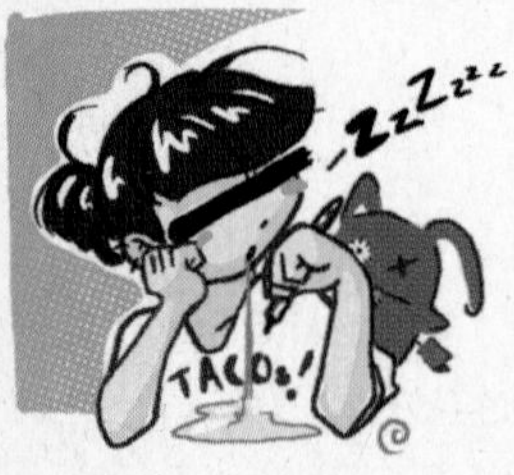
TACOs!

Christina C. Strain - Colorist

Christina is a lover of all things Zelda, the number one enemy of all things Taco, 50% narcoleptic, 50% hyper, and always, ALWAYS surrounded by her trusty friends UGLYDOLL and Pooh. When not coloring, or falling asleep while coloring, Christina dreams about how she will one day return to playing Ragnarok Online and FINALLY make her poor pink haired puncholyte into a full fledged battle priest.

Special thanks go out to the original series letterer, VC's Randy Gentile and digest letterer, Dave Sharpe.